The Dryden Press

Publications in Psychology

GENERAL EDITOR

THEODORE M. NEWCOMB

UNIVERSITY OF MICHIGAN

Children and Other People

ACHIEVING MATURITY THROUGH LEARNING

BY ROBERT S. STEWART

San Francisco State College

AND ARTHUR D. WORKMAN

HOLT, RINEHART AND WINSTON
NEW YORK

Copyright 1956 by Holt, Rinehart and Winston, Inc.

All rights reserved.

136. 7

St 4c

43, 915

Oct. 1962

FOREWORD

BY ERICH LINDEMANN, M.D.

Professor of Psychiatry, Harvard Medical School

OF ALL THE professionals who share the responsibility for the mental health of our children, the teacher has the most strategic role. Not only does he nurture the growing mind with information and skills; he also has the opportunity to watch over the child's emotional and social development. He can help the child to evolve a personality that is rich in interests and in capacity for human relationships. He can discover early signs of emotional impoverishment or tendencies toward delinquency or neurosis. And he can foster the kind of group life that will prepare the child for making all the creative contributions for which he is endowed.

Students and apprentices in the educational profession have long needed a book that sets forth clearly the best that is now known about personality development and emotional growth, that critically reviews the pertinent material in current literature, and that points out some of the unanswered questions in this fascinating field. But even more, young teachers need to develop fundamental orientations of their own, to be made cognizant of their own unsolved emotional problems, and to be helped to find ways of achieving greater emotional maturity and greater security *vis à vis* children and their parents.

It is their awareness of and attention to such needs that make the writers of the present book significant contributors to the teaching of education. I have had the great privilege of coming to know one of them, Dr. Robert Stewart, through his partici- pation in the Harvard-Wellesley Community Mental Health Study, which undertook to discover the part played by the schools in strengthening our children's growth toward mental health. As a psychiatrist, I have come to admire his profound insight into and understanding of the problems of teachers—both in the class- room and in their personal lives. This book represents a crystalli- zation of his wisdom.

The following pages contain a great deal of information about contemporary theory of personality development and the nature of emotional responses. But what is much more important is that this book gives the reader just the right combination of confidence and humility for tackling emotional and personality problems himself. Indeed, the book is so helpful that I hope it reaches not only teachers but members of other professions, such as church workers, nurses, and recreation leaders, who are involved deeply in the emotional problems of others. Parents also may gain from this book much-needed orientation toward the best contemporary thinking on safeguarding their children's mental health. The com- mon frame of reference which the authors provide should do much to unite parents and teachers in a mutually comfortable collaboration.

PREFACE

THIS BOOK is not intended to be definitive. We have tried to write a thought-provoking book, based upon our experiences and integrated with the thinking of others. We have made an effort to avoid technical jargon wherever possible, but where it has seemed necessary to do so, we have used words which may be unfamiliar to the reader. We have not reviewed, in this brief volume, a great many research studies, but, in the footnotes, we have tried to indicate to the interested reader where he can find such studies.

Our intentions have been to present the material in an organizational scheme that can be used flexibly. Although the contributions of Freud are discussed as early as Chapter 2, the book can be read by Freudians, non-Freudians, and anti-Freudians alike. We are indebted for our ideological and conceptual framework not only to Freud but also to Lewin, to living academic thinkers and practitioners, and even to writers of science fiction. But, in the last analysis, the book represents our thinking and our conclusions. We like to think that it is not a stew of eclecticism.

We have approached several ideas in several different ways. We have tried to convey Freud's thinking, for example, by means of verbal explanations of his concepts, by diagrams, and by case studies. We have attempted wherever possible to find the emotionally meaningful phrase and anecdote. However, we are firmly convinced that the most productive applications of the points we are making will come from discussions drawn from the reader's own life experience.

Finally, we wish to say—for the first but not the last time in this book—that we do not believe that the social sciences have reached the age of prescriptions. We do think that the way out of the brambles is becoming a little clearer because of clues, findings, methodology, and questions, and it is in this spirit that we have written.

R.S.S.
A.D.W.

Oakland, California
March 1956

ACKNOWLEDGMENTS

So many individuals have directly or indirectly contributed to this book in so many ways that it would be impossible to list all of them by name. We should like to thank all those with whom we have worked and studied, both children and adults, especially at the University of Wisconsin, the University of California, San Francisco State College, the Berkeley Public Schools, the Shasta and Modoc County Schools, the School of Public Health at Harvard University, and the Harvard-Wellesley Community Mental Health Study in Wellesley, Mass. We do want to single out two individuals who have been of inestimable and specific aid to us: our editor, Theodore M. Newcomb, and our publisher, Stanley Burnshaw.

CONTENTS

❦

PART ONE

INFANCY AND EARLY CHILDHOOD

❦

PART TWO

THE ELEMENTARY-SCHOOL YEARS

❧❧

PART THREE

ADOLESCENCE

❧❧

PART FOUR

EDUCATIONAL PSYCHOLOGY

PART FIVE
DISCIPLINE

PART SIX
THE PROBLEM CHILD

PART SEVEN
THE ADULTS AROUND THE CHILD

Children and Other People

Chapter 1

THE POINT OF VIEW

THE POINT of view of this book can be stated in relatively simple terms: the human organism is complex, and the principles of its organization are as yet only partially known to us; but the organism does have organization, and it is capable of change.

Under this principle are subsumed what to us appear to be hypotheses, postulates, and even axioms: At the outset, we offer these to the reader for two purposes: (1) for him to react to out of his total life experience in preparation for our presentation; and (2) as an overview of our book, and as a summary which he may reread after he has finished the book.

1. Children and adults are made out of the same psychological clay.

2. The adult differs from the child in that he has passed through various developmental stages, each of which has left a unique impression upon his personality.

3. In the formation of personality, the broad cultural environment, as well as the potential endowed by physical heredity, is in constant interaction with the familial environment.

4. More often than not, the human organism seems to have a

compulsion to survive, both psychologically and physically.

5. This compulsion, in view of a variety of external and internal counter forces, leads to a seeking for the "best way" of surviving.

6. What appears to be the "best way" to one individual may be or may seem to be a "bad way" to another.

7. Education, through teaching the skills, because of its social nature, and by virtue of the possible meaningfulness of the teacher, can contribute toward an individual's ease and productiveness in living.

8. This contribution is made not by "psychologizing" but by understanding the principles of growth and development, of educational practices, by recognizing the personality factors common to adults and children, and by having some applicable knowledge of the function of leadership.

9. "Rome was not built in a day," or by one person. By expecting miraculous, overnight changes in the behavior of children, teachers and parents may diminish their potential pleasure in their association with children.

10. The costs to adults of expecting such miracles are lessened warmth in their relations with children and lessened certainty concerning the direction their authority should take.

11. A major problem of human beings seems to us to be difficulty in and fear of feeling warm, intimate, and genuine.

12. Although all human beings seem to like to excel in whatever they attempt to do, all have certain limitations, and it is a sign of maturity to be able to call for and use appropriate help.

13. People live in groups—teachers and children, teachers and parents, teachers and teachers, parents and parents, children and children, parents and children, and so on *ad infinitum*. Important in the understanding of an individual is a knowledge of his relationships within groups.

We know relatively little today about how a personality develops, and the difficulties in describing what little we have discovered sometimes seem almost insurmountable. In the first place, the sum is not equal to its parts. A plus B does not equal C, for a multitude of relationships play a role in the process of becoming what we become. These relationships are not simple, mechanistic, or constant. Take, for example, so-called "parental rejection" (*i.e.*, the parents do not like their child). In actuality, it assumes many different forms and has many different consequences. It can be expressed by physical violence or be concealed behind a cloak of superficial sweetness. It can be conscious or unconscious, or both.

It is a temptation to try to diagram the process of personality formation, and we have made an attempt to do so (see pp. 50-62). But even the best diagram is unable to show fully the dynamic nature of the process, and furthermore it runs the danger of becoming cluttered by the almost infinite number of factors involved.

Fortunately, however, we have some basis for making deductions about the formation of personality. Although our knowledge is not yet precise, it has enough empirical validation to enable those in the social sciences to use it as a basis for prediction and for action.

A dramatic example of both our knowledge and our ignorance is the concept *psychosomatic*. We observe daily that emotional conditions have physical consequences. From such observations, we have come to recognize that the reactions of our bodies may react just as violently to emotional states as to germs or viruses. Our noses can run without our having a "cold" or allergy; we cry when we are sad; our breathing becomes short when we are uneasy. A growing mass of evidence indicates that there are still more subtle relationships between physical and emotional states. Yet we do not know whether there is a line of demarcation between *psyche* (the mind) and *soma* (the body), and, if it exists, where it is. We are, in short, in medicine and psychology, still puzzling over the ancient problem of the nature of the human organism. Is there a dichotomy between mind and body, or is the human organism one whole?

It is not our purpose, however, to immobilize the reader by describing the enormity of the questions involved. Rather, we wish to indicate at the outset the complexity of the problems which we shall consider, first, to discourage the reader from over-simplifying, and therefore ceasing to learn from his experience; and, second, to emphasize the fact that the child in the classroom is not static. He is the object of diverse influences, both past and present, and he is continually changing.

What is more, each person is unique. An I.Q. of 125 does not mean the same thing in two individuals. A disease, even though it has the same outward symptoms, does not affect two people in exactly the same way. One man will react quite differently from another to a gastric upset of the same degree and kind.

To cite an obvious example, John, born in March 1948, is a different person from Jim, born at the same time. Both have in common the characteristics of the species.[1] Both have in common their American heritage. They may also have similarities because their parents have like cultural backgrounds, attitudes toward child rearing, and so on. But there are both gross and subtle differences in the specific heredity and in the specific configurations (patterns of relationships) within the family of each boy. We have listed only a few of the forces that make for similarities and differences.

In a class of, say, thirty-five children, therefore, there are enough similarities among the individual pupils so that, for all

[1] For an amplified discussion of this point, see Henry A. Murray and Clyde K. Kluckhohn (eds.), *Personality in Nature, Society, and Culture* (Knopf, 1949), Part I.

practical purposes, they can be said to constitute a group. This means that on many occasions the teacher can treat them without differentiating one from another. On the other hand, the teacher should also bear in mind that, if either discipline or teaching the skills is to be effective, each individual needs in some ways to be differentiated from his peers. And most teachers encounter a few pupils who have been subjected to such special influences in the past that they require far different, even more individuated treatment.

To trace the development of a personality, to try to discover what makes it unique within the common framework, is a fascinating and difficult undertaking. The personality of the parents must be considered—their attitude toward themselves and toward each other, their economic status and their feelings about it, and the role that their children play in their lives. This means examining two people with personalities that are themselves unique, living in a particular time in history, with a particular set of values.

Even the world climate must be considered, for depression and prewar, wartime and postwar stresses all produce somewhat different family attitudes.

The child's sex and order of birth (whether he is the first, middle, or last child) also has significance. How the child has been fed, bowel- and bladder-trained, and how he is loved by both parents contribute to the molding of his personality.

Not only must the attitudes of the immediate family—mother, father, and siblings—be considered but also those of the extended family—grandparents, aunts, uncles, and cousins. A child who is the apple of his grandparents' eyes is going to be something different from a child who is compared unfavorably to other grandchildren.

Mrs. Jones, who lives next door, may also be an influence. The mores of the neighborhood and of the culture are of un-

questioned significance. Fighting is frowned upon in one neighborhood and approved in another; cleanliness is encouraged in
one part of town and ignored in another.[2] Of course, as the
child grows older, not only Mrs. Jones but also her children
affect his development. He learns about rivalry, power, friendship, and relations between the sexes from his playmates.

As he goes through school, many influences encroach upon
him. New authority figures in the guise of teachers appear; they
may become objects of fear or ideals after which he models
himself, or they may have some other psychological meaning
for him. He is now confronted with the task of formally learning certain skills that the culture requires, and his success or
failure, ease or difficulty, boredom or interest in these tasks may
have lasting effects. His family, though not so direct or exclusive
an influence as formerly, is never far in the background. Its
attitude toward school may have a positive or negative effect.

It can never be repeated too often that teachers are crucial
factors in the development of a child's personality, second only
to parents in this respect. For many years, most young children
spend more waking time with the teacher than with any other
one adult.

As the child enters the period of puberty, physiological
changes begin to take place. He is exposed to the same diversity
of influence as in his earlier years, but his receptivity to influence is different. Culture and his body are forcing him to take
a large step toward independence in establishing himself as an
adult member of the community. For many young people, this
is a period of confusion as they try to sort out and integrate
external and internal pressures.

The effect of the world situation upon the individual during
this period in his development is particularly striking. Jobs may

[2] See W. Allison Davis and Robert J. Havighurst, *Father of the Man* (Houghton Mifflin, 1947).

be easy to get, in which case he may find himself making more money than his teacher; the country may be at war, in which case he may be drafted (or her boyfriend may be drafted). Such circumstances can have great effect on the development of personality. The individual's stability and his confidence in planning for the future are all interrelated with the world climate. Its effect on delinquency, for example, and on school drop-outs is cardinal.[3]

Whatever the effect of such external influences, during these adolescent years, the individual is solving or attempting to solve the conflict that plagues all of us always to a greater or lesser degree—the conflict between our desire to be taken care of and our desire for freedom. How the child resolves this conflict and integrates these wants depends not only upon his past but also upon his present psychological, social, and physical environment.

During these transitional years between childhood and adulthood, the individual engages in much trial and error in behavior in an attempt to find the role best suited to his times and to himself. There is some disorganization and casting out of old ways of behaving before the ultimate reorganization and solidification of the personality takes place.

What we are attempting to do in this chapter is simply to suggest some of the intricacies that will be examined in more detail throughout this book. We ask the reader not to lay this book aside because he cannot at this point see the relevance of all this to child rearing and education. It may be helpful if he thinks of himself as not unlike an able general medical practitioner. Such a doctor is aware of the complexity of the problems he faces and of his limitations of time and knowledge; yet he

---

[3] For a discussion of the effect of socioeconomic and cultural conditions upon individual behavior, see *Now Hear Youth: A Report of California Cooperative Study of High School Drop-outs and Graduates* (California State Department of Education, 1953).

must work, expediently and by trial and error, with the tools available to him. Likewise, the teacher, recognizing that children have their difficulties, will at the outset teach at least groups of them by common methods. If the common methods fail in some cases or with some individuals, he will try to find methods that will succeed in those cases or with those individuals. If the standard method doesn't work, he will try a more specific remedy. As he grows in experience, he will, like the general practitioner, have at his disposal more and more ways of dealing efficiently with the exceptional. *And if he has some familiarity with the process of personality formation, he will often be able to avoid simple trial-and-error methods of finding a solution.* He will be aware of certain cause-and-effect relationships. What we have said here certainly applies to the parent as well as to the teacher.

It should also be emphasized that the teacher cannot be equally effective with all children. The exceptional child or the child with a strongly negative background from a mental hygiene point of view requires special treatment that few classroom teachers are equipped or trained to provide. In such cases, the teacher will need to call for help from other professionals with the time or training necessary to deal with such children. It is unfortunate that there are still many teachers who are reluctant to ask for help from the principal or supervisor or guidance worker. Yet all of us, no matter what our capacity, meet individuals and situations that are beyond our scope. Even the psychotherapist, operating in what appears to be an ideal situation since time and group needs are relatively unimportant, encounters patients with whom he does not succeed.

We have tried, in this chapter, to raise some fundamental questions, which we shall explore in the chapters that follow. The reader may wish to study the child's chronological development first, in which case he will read Chapters 2-7, on the Freudian contribution, and Chapters 8-13 on the elementary-school and adolescent years. He may, on the other hand, prefer to begin with the child in his social setting (Chapters 19-23), or with educational psychology (Chapters 14-18), or with the problem child (Chapters 24-26). Whatever section he reads first, he will be confronted in some way or another with the questions that we hope we have provoked in this chapter.

PART ONE

Infancy and Early Childhood

Chapter 2

THE FREUDIAN VIEW

~~~~~~

SIGMUND FREUD was born in 1856 and died in 1939.[1] Trained originally as a neurologist, he had a relatively uneventful practice in Vienna until, in the 1890's, he became increasingly interested in psychology. His discovery that hysterical patients (for example, those having paralysis without organic cause) could be successfully treated by being guided in an examination of the emotional roots of their disturbances led Freud to embark upon a long and thorough analysis of his own personality. As the result of his self-analysis, he began to formulate a theory of personality and of psychotherapy. His findings constitute the most revolutionary contribution to date toward understanding the human personality.

We do not mean to imply, by devoting several chapters to Freud and his ideas, that only he has contributed to psychology and psychiatry. Jung,[2] Adler, and Rank, Freud's contemporaries and at one time his disciples, have gone on to found "schools" of

[1] See Ernest Jones's revealing and readable biography, *The Life and Work of Sigmund Freud*, Vols. I (Basic Books, 1953) and II (Basic Books, 1955).
[2] See *Time*, Feb. 14, 1955, for a description of Jung's current point of view.

their own, as have such later therapists as Harry Stack Sullivan, Karen Horney, and Erich Fromm.[3] Yet the starting point for all these theorists was the work of Freud.

We cannot, of course, ignore the contributions of such research workers and theoreticians as William McDougall, John Dewey, and William James. We have emphasized Freud because we feel that his has been the greatest single impact upon all the behavioral sciences—not only psychology and psychiatry, but also sociology, education, and anthropology.

Clyde Kluckhohn has expressed the importance cf Freud's contribution to anthropology as follows:

For all of the extravagant dogmatism and pretentious impressionism of much psychoanalytic writing, the anthropologist sensed that here at last he was getting what he had long been demanding from academic psychology: a theory of raw human nature. . . . The anthropologist was positive that the theory was culture-bound to an important degree, though the evidence of the past twenty years indicates that many anthropologists exaggerated the extent of distortion they thought produced by bourgeois Viennese culture and by late-nineteenth-century science. At all events, psychoanalysis provided anthropology with a general theory that was susceptible to cross-culture testing by empirical means and with clues that might be investigated as the psychological causes of cultural phenomena.[4]

In effect, Kluckhohn is saying that Freudian theory (psychoanalysis) provides a base, which did not exist before, upon which theory and research in many social sciences can rest firmly.

For many years, however, psychoanalysis was in many circles a disreputable word. It was not until the 1930's that Freud became recognized by the medical and academic worlds. Since

---

[3] For a discussion of the thinking of these individuals and of their deviations from Freud, see Ruth L. Munroe, *Schools of Psychoanalytic Thought* (Dryden, 1955).

[4] Clyde Kluckhohn, "An Anthropologist Looks at Psychology," *American Psychologist*, Oct. 1948, pp. 439-442. Reprinted by permission.

many of the criticisms leveled against him had some validity, let us examine them.

At a time when psychology was striving to break away from philosophy and armchair speculation, Freud was considered regressive in that his studies of human nature were qualitative (*i.e.*, based upon careful observation of individuals) rather than quantitative and statistical. Actually, as an astute and creative observer of human behavior, Freud presented a number of hypotheses which were validated by the experience of other practitioners and, today, by the traditional scientific methods.

A second criticism was that Freud did not take sufficiently into account cultural influences upon personality and that he tended to see physical needs and impulses as constant in their manifestations, regardless of the societal setting. In other words, it was charged Freud believed that these physical needs and impulses operated in a cultural vacuum, so to speak, and therefore created the same problems the world over. In his last book,[5] as well as in earlier books, Freud took cognizance of these cultural factors. Many culturally oriented thinkers who accept his basic postulations have found it easy to elaborate his theory.[6]

Perhaps the most significant objection to Freud was leveled at his contention that sexual drives are of primary significance in the formation of personality. Sex was and is a touchy subject for discussion. It is not surprising that many people have refused to listen to what Freud has to say because his theory cannot be divorced from sexuality. As we shall attempt to show in this chapter, however, Freud's concept of sex, or of libidinal drives, was far more complex than the conventional one.

The controversy about Freud still goes on, though with less

[5] *An Outline of Psychoanalysis* (Norton, 1949).
[6] Clara Thompson and Patrick Mullahy, in *Psychoanalysis: Evolution and Development* (Hermitage, 1951), not only trace the historical development of Freudian theory but also analyze it from what might be called a "social" point of view.

fury than formerly. It would be useless to the purpose of this book to discuss the disagreements among Freudians, anti-Freudians, and "semi-Freudians." The point of view we wish to take is that his formulations have, to some degree, been integrated into much psychological thinking, and hence are worthy of examination by the teacher.

Kurt Lewin, a social scientist who made an enormous contribution in the direction of dynamically quantifying human behavior and analyzing the forces acting upon it, makes this judicious statement:

> . . . the psychoanalytic theory has developed a system *of ideas* unequaled in richness. . . . Its method of case study has the advantage of revealing the intimate history of the individual and the deeper personality layers in a way unreached by other methods. The psychoanalytical method does not give those opportunities for testing laws which the experimental procedure provides. It is necessary to bring the problems involved to a decidedly higher level, conceptually. Above all it is necessary to distinguish historical and systematic problems and to eliminate historical answers to systematic questions. As the systematic and historical problems in psychology can finally be solved only by dealing with both together, cooperation of the two approaches might prove to be fruitful.[7]

This quotation is a tribute to Freud from a man who is for us of equal stature and whose thinking starts from quite different premises. The inference for us is that Freudian concepts are not doctrinaire and can be incorporated into diverse approaches to the study of human personality.

It is difficult to say which of Freud's ideas is the most important. His concept of determinism, although it is no longer startling, is still highly significant. Freud believed that emotional disturbances and deviations from the so-called norm of human

[7] "Psychoanalysis and Topological Psychology," *Bulletin of the Menninger Clinic*, July 1936, pp. 202-211. Reprinted by permission.

behavior are governed by laws of cause and effect, as surely as are physical disturbances. In brief, a person who is emotionally ill is no more and no less blamable than a person who has the measles. Neuroses and psychoses are not a result of willfulness or evil spirits. Punishment will not cure them, nor is it "deserved." Personality, whether "normal" or "abnormal," is determined by the interaction among heredity, the constitution of the individual, his drives, and the total environment, including his familial relationships.

The implications of this idea are enormous, for if behavior is determined, it can also be influenced. If a child who lies and steals is not possessed by the devil, it may be possible, by understanding the causes of his lying and stealing, to treat his symptoms. Just as many kinds of physical illness that were once thought to be brought on by fate and beyond man's powers are now both preventable and curable, so also may personality difficulties prove to be.

An equally significant idea is Freud's concept of the unconscious. He believed that we all have feelings and motivations of which we are not aware. They are rooted deeply in the past and if unacceptable are not permitted to arise to consciousness. Freud differentiated the *un*conscious from the *sub*conscious— the latter being a term generally applied to the feelings and motivations nearer to the surface or consciousness, and less deeply buried.[8]

The unconscious cannot be disregarded, because it is a powerful driving force. Indeed, if apparently irrational behavior is to be modified, it is necessary that the unconscious motivations be brought into consciousness and analyzed. This "analysis" of un-

---

[8] For a more detailed account of Freud's theories, see *The Basic Writings of Sigmund Freud* (Modern Library, 1938); Sigmund Freud, *A General Introduction to Psychoanalysis* (Liveright, 1943); and *The Collected Papers of Sigmund Freud* (first published in London by Anglobooks in 1925, *et seq.*)

conscious motivations is a basic part of Freudian psychotherapy (a method of treating emotional problems). Generally the patient is urged to voice to the psychotherapist *any* thought that comes to mind (this method is called *free association*). Through free association of ideas, previously unconscious thoughts come to the surface and hence can be analyzed.

The placing of feelings and thoughts in the unconscious, Freud labeled *repression*. This for him was quite different from *suppression*—that is, conscious prohibition of an act by an individual. To use a simple example to distinguish between these two terms, one could say that a person walking down the street could sensibly suppress (consciously forbid himself) his desire to pick a nice red apple off the fruit stand. On the other hand, if to this same person even the *desire* to take an apple were emotionally forbidding, the thought of taking the apple would "never enter his head," for the idea would remain in the unconscious—that is, be repressed.

Although repression plays a major role in emotional illness, it should be emphasized that it does not necessarily lead to emotional disturbances. Freud recognized that the prime necessity is to come to the best possible terms with life and reality and that there are times when it is necessary to place a buffer, so to speak, between oneself and ideas and feelings which are not tolerable. In other words, the human personality of necessity builds (to use the Freudian phrase) certain defense mechanisms as the best way of achieving psychological survival. There are a number of such mechanisms besides repression but they will be discussed in Chapter 25.

To give another example of the use of repression, a child utterly distressed by the death of a parent protects himself from his unbearable sorrow by repressing his feelings about the death. To do otherwise would be psychologically too distressing to himself. Outwardly, or consciously, he maintains an attitude of indifference, hiding from himself those feelings which are too painful. Callousness in children or in adults, which is often offensive to others, may be related to repression and if understood as such may be dealt with more effectively by teachers and parents.

One of the primary differences between psychotherapy and educational therapy from our point of view is that in psychotherapy the defenses may be examined in a special environmental setting and with a person especially trained for this. In the classroom the teacher may make an effort to provide so secure an environment that the defenses may not be needed, but he does not deal with them directly. They have a purpose and should not be tampered with except by or in collaboration with the proper specialist.

As can be seen, Freud recognized the complexity of the personality and in an attempt to understand this complexity divided personality into three parts, which he named the *id*, the *ego*, and the *superego*. Each term is difficult to define because it interacts with and overlaps the others. Perhaps the most effective way to describe them would be to give an overview of their genesis. When the infant is born, no ego or superego exists. He is in a sense "all id"—that is, he is an organism compounded of drives, impulses, or instincts of a biological nature which seek satisfaction or gratification, mainly through eating. These drives, which have some of the qualities of energy, Freud called the *libido*. In the second and third years, the libido is directed toward gratification of pleasures connected with elimination. In the fourth and fifth years and later stages of development, the major object of the libido, or id, is satisfaction of the sexual impulses as these are generally understood.

Toward the end of the first year the infant gradually and dimly comes to differentiate between himself and other persons. Those who have observed very small children will readily be aware that as time goes on the child becomes a person. He develops a sense of self, of "I-ness." This Freud calls the ego.

As his parents or equivalent authorities make certain prohibitions, particularly during the period when he is being bowel- and bladder-trained, a sense of what is right and wrong begins to grow. He develops a conscience which forbids him under certain conditions to gratify his id, or pleasure-seeking impulses. This conscience Freud termed the superego.

Thus, we can speak of a strong ego or a weak ego, meaning a strong sense of self and an ability to estimate the reality in which one lives. Theoretically, the ego is dominated by the urge for preservation within any particular culture. Ideally, therefore, it maintains a balance between id and superego that is healthful for the person.

These concepts are difficult to explain because they cannot truly be compartmentalized. The id, the ego, and the superego are not specific areas of the body but are words used to describe impulses and ways of communication with oneself and others. Seldom if ever do these aspects of the total personality exist by themselves. They actually interact, reenforcing or controlling one another.

An understanding of the central role of sex and of the presence of this force in young children was another of Freud's major contributions. If we are able to divest sex of the taboos that surround it, we can see that adult adjustment, including sexual adjustment, is directly related to child-rearing practices—and we can also see the significance of this fact. To make our point clear, however, it will be necessary to examine in some detail the three phases of psychosexual development which Freud believed all children pass through. We shall begin this discussion with the next chapter.

Chapter 3

FEEDING AND
WEANING

I т is Freud's contention that the infant's introduction to the world about him centers around feeding, and that this introduction is a crucial one. Upon it depends to an extremely significant degree the child's feelings toward himself and toward others as well as a healthy beginning of his sexual development. [1]

The mother communicates much to the child when she nurses him. Her feelings toward him are conveyed at this time. She can be fully accepting (having affection for him) or rejecting (disliking him) or she may have feelings between these extremes, and these feelings may be conscious, unconscious, or both. If the mother, as she becomes confident in her capacity to be a mother, enjoys motherhood to a greater rather than lesser degree, she feels naturally warm toward the infant. Hence, the child starts life in an emotional atmosphere conducive to security.

We want to emphasize that it is the mother's basic and per-

---

[1] Erik Erikson reviews and re-examines child development from a Freudian viewpoint in *Childhood and Society* (Norton, 1950).

vasive feelings that are significant. Every mother is likely to have moments or days of irritability, and hence no mother is always serene and affirmative in her feelings toward her baby. But these transitory negative feelings do not necessarily have an adverse effect upon the child's psychological growth. When these feelings cease to be transient, however, the danger signals may be raised.

Spitz has given us rather convincing evidence that continued emotional deprivation can result in retardation of intellectual development.[2] In research reported by him, mothers individually attended their illegitimate infants during the first six months of life and the infants developed normally. After this period, the mothers left and the children remained in an orphanage, well cared for in terms of diet and physical hygiene but with relatively little emotional contact with adults. Developmental rate slowed, and in several years actual retardation became apparent.

The assumption, then, is that through the close, warm, friendly relationship between mother and child a healthy personality can be established during the first year of life.

Undoubtedly many aspects of the mother-child relationship contribute toward the building of a healthy personality. However, the focal point for Freud is feeding—both manner and method. For many years psychoanalysts strongly advocated breast feeding. It was thought that breast feeding under optimal conditions, because of the close bodily contact, was the best way of communicating these feelings. Breast feeding may be psychologically contraindicated, however, if it is distasteful to the mother, for if such an attitude exists the child may receive a feeling of resentment. The really important thing is not whether the child is breast- or bottle-fed but how the mother feels toward him

[2] René Spitz's research is reported in the *Psychoanalytic Study of the Child* (International Universities), Vol. I, and his research has also been filmed under the title *Genesis of Emotions*, distributed by New York University.

and his feeding.[3] These feelings are reflected in how she holds him and cuddles him while he is feeding and whether he is allowed to satisfy both his hunger and his pleasure in sucking.

Surprisingly much is also communicated to the child through the apparently simple matter of the scheduling of the feeding. There was a time, around 1930, when both pediatricians and psychologists advocated in no uncertain terms that infants should be trained as rapidly as possible to eat at regular intervals, ordinarily every four hours. Today it seems strange that anyone ever believed that all babies should invariably become hungry every four hours and, furthermore, hungry for a given quantity, when no two adults have the same kind of appetite or eat the same amount of food at the same hours every day.

Stated simply, the position was that desirable adult characteristics could be produced by rigid and consistent conditioning. Thus, if a child were to become a "well-regulated adult"—eating three meals a day at proper hours, never displaying unhappiness, and having one bowel movement daily at the right time—his conditioning had to begin early. Hungry and voracious infants had to wait until the clock permitted them to eat, whereas the less forthright child was fed at the appointed time regardless of his appetite. Mothers were admonished, when their infants cried, to see whether they were being stuck by safety pins and if not, to leave them alone. It is difficult to tell whether this was harder on the infant or the family.

There is now abundant evidence from research that contradicts this interpretation.[4] We are reasonably sure that children learn

[3] Benjamin Spock, in *Pocket Book of Baby and Child Care* (Pocket Books, 1946), presents in simple language the pediatrician's current view on the whole problem.

[4] Arthur T. Jersild, in *Child Psychology*, 3d ed. (Prentice-Hall, 1941), Chap. III, reports much fascinating research on "the eating education" of children. A research on feeding that points in an anti-Freudian direction is reviewed by Harold Orlansky, "Infant Care and Personality," *Psychological Bulletin*, Jan. 1949, pp. 1-48.

most rapidly when they reach a given psychological and physiological point for the particular learning. We are also reasonably sure that behavior changes for many reasons, including those of growth and of environment, and that a given behavior does not persist simply because it holds sway at one stage of life. Therefore, neither simple repetition nor earliness in training insures results and, in fact, prematurity may have deleterious effects.

Interestingly enough, children who are fed on what is now commonly called a demand basis (that is, when they are hungry) soon seem, as a group, to establish reasonably regular schedules for themselves—often every four hours—and voluntarily to give up night feeding. Nevertheless, one of the psychological advantages of a demand schedule is that it allows for individual differ· ences and for differences in the same individual on different days. With this flexibility, unnecessary frustration is not introduced.

This term *frustration* has been much bandied about in recent years and perhaps misunderstood. Because psychologists have recognized that in certain circumstances frustration can be detrimental, some teachers and parents believe that they must at any cost make the child's life frustration-free.

If frustration is defined as a barrier or obstacle in the way of the satisfaction of needs and wishes, it can be readily seen that a life without frustration is an impossibility. One of the challenges of parenthood, therefore, becomes that of teaching the child how best to meet frustration. This education begins during the oral period (the first year of life, when the emotional point of concentration is feeding) and can be related both to the schedule of feeding and to weaning.

We make two assumptions. First, if the child is expected to comply with requirements which are too far beyond his psychological and physiological capacities, his security may be undermined. Secondly, if he is unrealistically overprotected, he may not learn how to tolerate frustration. Problems relating to frustration appear throughout all the formative years, and they first appear during the oral period.[5]

Specifically during the first year the infant should ordinarily be fed, all things being equal, at those times when he is hungry. However, as Spock has said, it is absurd for the mother to feel compelled to feed the child at the very moment of his first hunger cry. The mother who abruptly terminates her telephone conversation immediately when her child cries, for fear lest the infant be frustrated, is creating in a different way as unfavorable a situation as the mother who plugged her ears during the last half hour before the infant was scheduled to be fed. The latter mother may be conveying feelings of rejection, but the former mother may be on her way to rearing an "overprotected" child.

It might be pointed out at this time that although the increasing knowledge of child development is all to the good, it is also unfortunate that preoccupation with the psychology of child rearing has led some people to underestimate the resilience of the human organism. The age-old tendency to swing from extreme to extreme never seems to die. One is correctly suspicious of the desirability of sending children out selling newspapers at the age of four. Yet it is doubtful that children are, as one public lecturer once told parents, like delicate watches. They are both tender and tough.

The more accurate analogy is probably that the human personality is like a tomato plant. The seed germinates best under extremely protected conditions (like the embryo in the womb). The seedling is kept in an even-temperatured room and watered with great care, in accordance with its vital needs. In due time, when proper strength is achieved, the plant is set outdoors (because for healthy development it needs a more natural rather than

[5] The role of frustration in everyday child rearing is aptly discussed by Dorothy Barclay in "Home Discipline," *New York Times Magazine*, May 25, 1952.

a greenhouse environment). It is still protected against excessive heat or rain, but the gardener, recognizing that there is a toughness that increases as the plant grows and that this is healthy, does not overnurture it. He realizes, in brief, that a plant subjected to more stress than it can bear will either wither and die or be spindly and barren, and that a plant kept permanently in a greenhouse will produce insipid fruit and will be vulnerable to such adversities as nature introduces.

Just as frustration can contribute to or defeat the growth of a plant, so does it play a crucial role in the growth of the human organism. Of course, one should not extend the analogy too far. In human beings the feelings toward frustration are what count, and how one feels about frustration dictates how one handles it.

Not only through the schedule of feeding but also through the nature of weaning, the child learns to meet frustration. Weaning is truly his first encounter with having to give up what he wants. At one time some psychologists advocated that the child was to be weaned (that is, from breast or bottle to the cup) very early in the first year and suddenly. Pediatricians went so far as to insist that the weaning be accomplished in a single day by simply withholding the bottle from the infant until he became hungry enough to eat from the cup. It was truly a Spartan point of view. Unfortunately, although the immediate objective may have been attained, the price was often great for sensitive parents and for the child. The child, if he succumbed, did so at a cost; he may have developed an outwardly compliant but inwardly resentful feeling. Furthermore, regression (reverting to earlier modes of behavior) was not uncommon. The desire for sucking, if thwarted prematurely, sometimes manifests itself later on in more thumb sucking than is commonly expected, for example.

Psychoanalysts, as well as representatives of other points of view, now emphasize that weaning should be gradual. Observation and research strongly indicate that the child who is weaned gradually and when he is ready for weaning gives up the bottle without great reluctance. He may, for security purposes, want it at night for a couple of years, but this does not prevail forever.

This does not mean that even with the most correct feeding and weaning, the child will never resort to sucking. There seems to be a close connection between security and putting something into one's mouth either for sucking or eating. The more tense and stressful the situation and the individual, the greater is the tendency to place something in the mouth. When faced with a scolding or a difficult school task, children of school age will choose almost anything, from fingers to pencils. Teachers (behind closed doors, of course) smoke, chew gum, eat candy, consume more coffee or tea than they are physically hungry for, or even drink three martinis instead of the usual one when they are uneasy.

The point we are making is that eating and sucking provide security. If the child is unduly deprived of these activities, bases may be laid for later insecurity. But human beings, no matter how "well adjusted" they are, tend to resort to what are called "oral satisfactions" when insecure.

In summary of what we have said thus far, during the oral period the human personality has its first lessons in feeling security and in meeting frustration. Mainly through the way in which he is fed, the infant comes to feel the world as friendly or unfriendly, himself as loved or unloved, and hence, other human beings as lovable or unlovable. Being lovingly and well fed provides the first contribution to a sureness that the world is not too forbidding. Being fed reasonably close to the time he is hungry and being weaned gradually and when he is ready teach him to deal with frustration without excessive tension.

Finally, from the Freudian position, we must note that sexual attitudes also have their genesis at this time. As was pointed out in the preceding chapter, Freud believed that adult sexual adjustment was related to the ways in which the child's various physiological needs were satisfied or controlled at the several stages of his psychosexual development. Thus, during the oral period the libidinal drives (embryonic sexual impulses) are focused around eating. If feeding is pleasurable, the basis may be present for later acceptance without guilt of other physiological pleasures. Contrariwise, if eating is unpleasant, it may be the basis for unpleasant associations with physiological satisfactions in adult life. Moreover, Freud thought that adult sexuality, which includes both love and sensuality, grows out of the first love—the love of the mother for her infant—an idea which, if one divests sexuality of its guilt-laden implications, is really a conventional one.

Chapter 4

TOILET TRAINING

THE ORAL PERIOD ends at some time near the close of the first year of life, and the child is next confronted with the truly formidable physiological and psychological problem, imposed by his mother and the culture, of bowel- and bladder-control. Although the child is obviously learning many other things at this time, it is the bowel- and bladder-training that may produce extreme tensions in the parent and in the child. Freud called this stage of psychosexual development the *anal* period.[1]

It is interesting to note how charged with emotion the function of elimination is for many people. One of the barriers to the acceptance of Freudian theories is the very fact that he concerned himself with this subject and gave to this phase of development what is to many people a repugnant name.

It is significant that discussion of the functions of elimination is thought to be indecent and at the same time, either in dis-

---

[1] The reader who would like to know more about Freud's concept of child development may find the following books stimulating: Anna Freud, *Psychoanalysis for Teachers and Parents* (Emerson, 1935); and Oliver S. English and G. H. J. Pearson, *Emotional Problems of Living* (Norton, 1945).

guised or open form, is highly compelling. Among some individuals exchange of information about frequency, times, and methods of securing "proper" elimination becomes almost clinical. More often reference to elimination must be hidden by humor. In fact, it is perhaps one of the most productive sources of "dirty jokes."

Beneath the humor seems to lie shame. The genesis of this shame appears to be very early. There are children who are so timid about relieving themselves at school that they exercise extraordinary control to postpone it until they get home. Not a few adults find it difficult when at a party or in a strange place to ask about the location of the toilet.

Humor helps here, since we evidently find it difficult to use the correct name for the room where we eliminate. People ask where the "bathroom" is when they have no intention of taking a bath. Euphemisms are many, and they appear to be more acceptable than the appropriate words. College students, as well as others, refer to the "john," "latrine," and "head," and it has just come to our attention that some people prefer to use the "sandbox." Filling stations in some areas have "He" and "She" on what are called "restrooms" (without even a hard-backed chair in them), and at one college with which we are familiar there is a "Ladies' Parlor" which the female students say is an extremely barren place.

Not only where we do it but what we do has many names. This can cause confusion for small children if "Number One" and "Number Two" interchange their meaning in different locales. A child who has been taught to say he has "to do business" or "to tinkle" may puzzle an adult unfamiliar with the usage. It may be hard to believe but we once ran across an otherwise intelligent registered nurse who asked adult patients, without cracking a smile, if they had to "wee-wee."

This attraction to and avoidance of the subject of elimination is considered as evidence in support of the Freudian point of view that this function is emotionally charged and that hence bowel- and bladder-training of the child plays a major role in the formation of personality.

This intensity of feeling on the part of parents places a weapon in the child's hands. On first glance—and perhaps even on fifth glance to some—this may seem to be farfetched. But consider the emphasis that many parents place upon not only the control but also the regularity of elimination. All of us, we suspect, have known mothers who have gone to great pains to reward or to punish a child in order to induce regularity. They play games, make noises like a locomotive, and frown or smile, depending upon the production or its absence. It is not surprising, then, that if the parents are so preoccupied, the child soon learns (unconsciously and sometimes consciously) that he can give pleasure or create anxiety by either giving or withholding in this respect; in short, he has a weapon.

Of course, children do not find it necessary to wield this power if relations with the mother have been more pleasant than unpleasant during the oral period. If these relations continue during the bowel- and bladder-training, the child will tend to do what the mother wants because of the pleasure of pleasing her. Or— even more desirable—he will learn as do the Navajo, by imitation; *i.e.*, he will use the toilet because he has observed that his parents use the toilet.[2]

It is Freud's contention that conscience (concepts and attitudes toward right and wrong) begins to develop during the anal period. Harshness of the training may predispose toward harsh conscience. The rigid external demands of the parents may contribute toward the development in the child of a rigid and fearful

[2] Clyde K. Kluckhohn and Dorothea Cross Leighton, in *Children of the People* (Harvard, 1937), report on and analyze child-rearing practices among the Navajos. The reader may be interested in this psychological-anthropological study and its implications.

conscience. An absence of any kind of intervention with natural impulses might predispose toward an absence of conscience or, as Freud called it, super-ego. If the parents were prey to the child's manipulation during the bowel- and bladder-training period, another alternative (and these are obviously very generalized statements) might be a development of conscience and a sense of self which conceives successful interpersonal relations as being based on manipulation.

It must be emphasized again that the ultimate personality depends upon the pattern of parent-child relationship over a period of years and that no one period definitively determines the personality. We are simply stating that we are inclined to believe that the manner in which the child is bowel- and bladder-trained contributes significantly toward his behavioral pattern in later life.

Freud, himself, is quite specific about the relationship between particular adult personality characteristics and the adult's childhood bowel- and bladder-training. Thus, he would trace the origin of compulsive giving (having continually to give presents, etc.) in an adult to the necessity of conforming during the anal period if he were to be loved by his parents. The gifts do not have to be material things: they can be affection, agreeableness, aid, or words. We have all met, for example, people who must flatter to the point of embarrassment. The assumption here is that they are afraid that they will lose love unless they give. Conversely, children who were successfully coaxed into conforming may as adults give "their favors" and their affections only when coaxed or may give only with reluctance. Freud found other fascinating variations of adult personalities and felt they paralleled quite closely the kind of interpersonal relations that obtained with the parents during the bowel- and bladder-training period.

The problem of teaching bowel- and bladder-control has much

in common with that of weaning. Too early training may result in regressions later on or may be emotionally too costly for the child. The university research workers who have extensively studied and observed child growth and development [3] report that the child learns best when he is physically, intellectually, and emotionally at the maturation point for a particular learning. Therefore, the parent who attempts to teach bowel- and bladder-control prematurely (that is, before *about* the first birthday) may be wasting his time. If he succeeds in intimidating the child enough to achieve success, he may be contributing to the formation of an overcontrolled individual. Such a person, as an adult, *must* always conform and is afraid of natural impulses and spontaneity.

It is Freudian theory that the kind of cleanliness and neatness that goes beyond the ordinary requirements of social living—the kind that drives not only the housewife herself but her whole family to distraction—is related to the housewife's severe bowel- and bladder-training—to her learning the hard way and prematurely to control a function that was designated as dirty and unclean. Certainly compulsiveness about neatness, cleanliness, time, and organization can reach the point where it interferes with rather than contributes to effective living. There is simply no reasonable reason for a teacher to stay half an hour after school, missing her bus, in order to see that every pin is in place when she is coming down with the flu and would be better off at home.

On the other hand, there are personalities who avoid and evade any kind of restrictions. They find it very difficult, if not impossible, to delay pleasure, presumably because their bowel-

[3] We again refer the reader to Arthur T. Jersild, *Child Psychology* (Prentice-Hall, 1941), who reviews with great care the research on this phase of child development. The same author in Chap. 4 of the 4th edition of this work (1954) brings the thinking up to date.

and bladder-training was erratic or absent or done by parents who felt that any "frustration" would be harmful.

As we have pointed out, research has shown that for each child there is an opportune time for learning this control—that is, there is a time when he learns most efficiently and with the least cost to his personality. The exact time will differ for each child, depending in part upon physical growth. The control of sphincter muscles is not easy and requires relative maturation of the nervous system, which is reached after about two years of life. Equally important, controls are learned best when the parents can communicate to the child what they want done and why. The child can then understand and better respond. Hence, a child who can talk and tell the parent that he needs to void and who understands the parent's request will learn this control more easily. Moreover, because it is a complex learning, the control is learned best over a period of time, not suddenly or in a few weeks.

Studies indicate rather conclusively that trying to train a child by "catching" him at the right time results only in wear and tear on the mother's nervous system. "Natural" rhythms are established by training and are not present before training. Before he is trained, the "usual" child eliminates at different times on different days, depending upon diet and other factors.

Training that is achieved simply through the exertion of parental authority may be successful, but the emotional cost to both the parents and child may be too great. Moreover, not infrequently, "successful" training may turn out to be an illusion. Regression a year or two later or even more is not uncommon in children trained too early or too strictly. The mother is in despair to find herself right back where she started. Lack of daytime or nighttime control may reappear even after the fourth year and continue through adolescence, when it becomes much more complicated to deal with.

Enuresis (bed-wetting occurring after control has been established) is seldom caused by physical deformities, and pediatricians generally look first for psychological reasons. It may be, if the child was trained too punitively, a manifestation of rebellion, if in the later years he feels able to rebel. Enuresis may be a way of manipulating the parents because the parents have become so worried that the child is possessed of a real weapon. Sometimes a child who has attained control regresses because there is a new baby in the family or because the parents have outside interests. He finds that by bed-wetting he can gain the parents' recognition and concern, which he feels he has lost. Sometimes he learns that enuresis is a way of gaining rewards. One might question the effectiveness of paying a child for not wetting his bed. Any child (with shrewdness) would soon see that if he could earn a nickel a night he might be able to raise the ante to a dime by just having a few off nights, and so on *ad infinitum*.

Treating enuresis, therefore, should take into consideration causes, as should treating anything. Any particular method of treating a symptom may be doomed to failure if it does not reach the cause. Shaming, for example, seems often ineffective in dealing with enuresis. The child who is shamed may become over-anxious and have less control. In the long run, a symptom that is got rid of by banishment, not by removal of the cause, will only be replaced by another symptom.

In summary , the bowel- and bladder-training period is psychologically significant for these reasons: (1) the child learns that certain prohibitions against what one may impulsively want to do are imposed by social living; (2) he may learn these prohibitions too severely and may become a frightened or rebellious adult as a consequence; (3) he may learn that restrictions can contribute to social living if bowel- and bladder-control are achieved by nonfearsome parental authority; (4) raising once more the problem of frustration, first encountered during the oral period, bowel- and bladder-training may serve to help the child deal with obstacles in the path of his immediate wishes; (5) various adult personality patterns may be potentially established; the individual may learn to manipulate other people by withholding, offering tentatively, giving in order to purchase security, etc.

Lastly, it should be pointed out that adult feelings and attitudes toward sex are related to this phase of psychosexual development. It will be recalled that the libido during the oral period is directed toward sucking and eating. Weaning accomplished, libidinal drives center on functions of elimination. If during these two periods the child has found pleasure in his sensuality and yet learned to integrate and control it, he is well on the road to incorporating into his adult personality his sexual impulses, which appear in a more conventional form during his fourth year of life.

Chapter 5

SOCIALIZATION

Wɪᴛʜ the attainment of bowel- and bladder-control at about the end of the third year, the object of the libido becomes sexual gratification in its more usual sense—*i.e.*, via the genital area. This phase of psychosexual development is sometimes termed by Freud the *phallic period*.

However, since the resolution of what Freud called the Oedipal (parental) ties is the most crucial happening during this period, we prefer the name the *Oedipal period*. The Oedipal "complex" (which deals with these Oedipal ties) is not so fearsome as it may sound; it refers to the observable phenomenon that the boy develops a special attachment for his mother and the girl a special attachment for her father. The name Oedipus refers to the legend dramatized by the Greeks in which Oedipus Rex fatefully and unknowingly slays his father and marries his mother. (The attachment of daughter for father was called the Electra complex by Freud. However, this term is seldom used.[1])

[1] Patrick Mullahy, in *Oedipus: Myth and Complex* (Hermitage, 1948), traces critically the development of Freud's thinking on this period and includes in his book the *Oedipus*, a dramatic trilogy by Sophocles.

It is during the years of the Oedipus period that, in the simplest terms, the child continues to learn how to live with people, how to deal with them, how secure he can be with them and how they estimate him. His sexual drives are now integrally enmeshed in these relationships. Their mode of expression, their strength, and their direction have their genesis in how he accomplishes these learnings.

Freud's theory about this period is based on phenomena frequently observed by parents and teachers. Boys, when they are four or five years of age, become especially attached to their mothers and get crushes on their female teachers. At the same time they become antagonistic to and worshipful of (in almost equal parts) older males. These phenomena appear in reverse fashion with girls of this age.

To a greater or lesser degree most children pass to other attachments in later life, but it is also observable that some never seem to be able to break the intensity of this original tie with a parent of the opposite sex.

If the individual never outgrows the intense attachment to the parent of the opposite sex, he is said to have "an Oedipus complex." Such a pervasive attachment may interfere with the achievement of satisfactory extrafamilial (nonparental) relationships in later life. Ideally, Freud thought, both boys and girls learn during this period to develop affectional ties which are nondistressing with members of both the same and opposite sex. Obviously, such ties include sexual (genital) feelings, and whether these feelings are to become in maturity rejected, shameful, overdemanding, or integrated is in part a presumed outcome of this period.

It is difficult to estimate the impact of the Oedipal relationship upon the child's development. Not only are his gross attitudes toward sex influenced, but also many if not all of his interpersonal relationships with members of the same and the opposite sex, both those who are peers and those who are in authority positions.[2]

The objectives that Freud hoped would be achieved during the Oedipal period were: (1) facility in relating to members of the opposite sex; (2) pride in one's own sex; (3) ability to work with authorities without fear; (4) integration of the sexual impulses without guilt on the one hand or devouringness on the other (as in nymphomania or satyriasis).

Ideally, this comes about through the identification (the modeling after without competitiveness) of the child with the parent of the same sex. It is during this period that the child begins to recognize some of the behaviors and attitudes that the culture prescribes for the two sexes.

What specific personal and interpersonal problems does the child face during the Oedipal period? We think that three require detailed discussion: (1) sex play; (2) feelings toward the parent or parent substitute of the opposite sex; (3) feelings toward one's own sex and its value.

We shall first direct our attention toward sex play. Although self-manipulation and observation of both one's self and others appear earlier as well as later in a more or less sporadic manner, masturbation, curiosity about differences of biological structure, and pleasure in physical contact with others seem to reach a peak between the ages of four and six.[3]

As we point out in a later chapter, genital sexual interests wane

[2] The reader who wishes to study more thoroughly the interpersonal inferences of Freudian theory is referred not only to those works of Freud himself and those mentioned in previous footnotes but also to the works of Harry Stack Sullivan. Sullivan was particularly interested in adapting psychoanalytic theory in the "social" direction. Many of his major hypotheses will be found in Patrick Mullahy (ed.), *The Contributions of Harry Stack Sullivan* (Hermitage, 1952), and a summation of his theories appears in Dorothy R. Blitsten, *The Social Theories of Harry Stack Sullivan* (William-Frederick Press, 1953).
[3] See Arthur T. Jersild, *Child Psychology* (Prentice-Hall, 1954), for researches on children's sexual activities.

during the elementary-school years. Their appearance in acute form during late preschool and kindergarten years does not indicate that the child, male or female, is in any way exceptional. From Freud's point of view, the significance of sexual development lies in its psychological meaning: the child is learning to relate to members of both sexes, primarily through the usually most emotionally important people about him—his father and his mother.

The reader will recall that previously, and in correlation with physical growth and needs, the child was learning to relate to himself and others through feeding and bowel- and bladder-training. At about the fourth year his physical growth and his emotional needs tend to revolve around the genital feelings. The child is both physically and emotionally more sexually aware of other people, and his relationships with them become more sexually tinged for him. He becomes more caressing and loving, sometimes in a frank and sometimes in a secretive manner.

This development is sometimes distressing to parents and teachers who may overrespond to it (exploit it) or underrespond (giving the child a feeling of rejection). The parent or teacher, instead of being embarrassed or scolding, may make an important contribution to the child's development by understanding this "aggressive" sexual behavior as another phase of the child's learning to be himself with others.

The parents' attitude toward the child's sexual activities at this time determines to a large degree how he solves what we have termed his second major problem: his feelings toward the parent of the opposite sex. It is to this problem that we now wish to direct our attention.

For Freud, desirable and productive heterosexual relationships are more likely to appear in maturity if, during the Oedipal period, the child's gestures of affection are received naturally and easily by the parent of the opposite sex. Thus the just plain liking of a mother for her young son or a father for his young daughter will aid the child in establishing comfortable and secure relationships in later years with members of the opposite sex. On the contrary, a parent who is consciously or unconsciously unfriendly, retaliatory, or overpossessive of the child of the opposite sex may be complicating the child's natural progression through this phase of his development.

Of course, in real life there are many subtle variations in mother-son and father-daughter relationships. Some seem more productive of "good adjustment" in maturity than others, but we reiterate that the hypothetical and absolute ideal is rarely if ever seen. However, we are quite in agreement with John Levy and Ruth Munroe,[4] who maintain in essence that there are many kinds of "ideal" families.

To indicate the effects that varying kinds of parent-child Oedipal relationships may have upon personality development, we shall cite a few examples, drawn from cases with which we have worked:

Laura, a school teacher, age 29, had a father who wanted a boy child. In compensation, he turned Laura into a kind of son, taking her fishing and hunting while the mother stayed home, and teaching her how to repair automobiles. Laura enjoyed this companionship and the outcome seemed to be an ability to relate easily to men. At any rate she married a man who also liked camping and she averred how much fun her marriage was because she could share so many outdoor interests of her husband.

Here is an illustration of how one father-daughter relationship, which would seem to have produced an unhappily masculine woman because her father would have preferred a son, did not do so. We hypothesize that the father liked his little girl and reciprocated her liking him by being companionable along his own interest lines.

[4] John Levy and Ruth L. Munroe, *The Happy Family* (Knopf, 1938).

Then there was Ed:

Ed's mother never lived with her father, but only with relatives, who gave her more material goods than affection. Her uncle was the closest personification of a father. He exemplified for her the importance of the male as a breadwinner and as a means of gaining social status. She yearned for love but received no substance of it. Her attitude toward her own husband and toward her son Ed seems to reflect the instability of her relationship with her "father substitute." Ed was indulged, purchased, threatened, and not infrequently loved. The mood swings were so frequent, though, that he had little stability or self-discipline in either scholastic or social activities, being expelled from one school or scout troop after another. His treatment centered initially around creating a safe, even, personal relationship both for his mother and himself.

Ed illustrates, we think, how insecurity and conflicting attitudes of a mother toward her own father stimulate a feeling of uneasiness, hostility, and counterattack in the son, who is consciously or unconsciously the recipient of the mother's own bewilderment.

A case in which school difficulties seemed directly related to the mother-son relationship during the Oedipal period was that of Larry.

Larry's mother wanted a girl child. She had a boy instead, who turned out to be a handsome lad with large eyes and wavy hair. During his preschool and kindergarten years, his mother, with no malice intended, curbed his aggressive interests in boyish games, dressed him in short pants when other boys were wearing long khakis, let his hair grow in long ringlets, and took him to the symphony and poetry readings. Larry, at the age of eleven, was probably the "brightest" boy in his class but was also one of the most disliked, and certainly one of the most retiring and timid. He was miserable if he did not get the highest grades of anyone, was utterly inept in any sport, and tagged along after the girls but was not acceptable to them.

For us Larry illustrates a personality development that is at least in part the result of a mother-son relationship which, though kindly, was during the Oedipal period possessive in a particular kind of way. The mother wanted to create a son in her own image, so to speak, and tended to completely possess him when he was passing through the filial-attachment phase, rather than accepting him as a growing and increasingly independent male child.

These three samples have been selected at random to illustrate the influence of the relationship between the parent and the child of the opposite sex. Other influences obviously were at work. We caution the reader to remember that personality development is a consequence of many relationships (for example, those during the oral and those during the bowel- and bladder-training period) and, although what happened in each phase leaves its mark, none in itself is sufficient to explain why a person becomes a particular kind of personality.

The reader will recall that we enumerated three major specific problems the child faces between the years of four and six. We have discussed the first two and now will approach the third: the feelings of the child toward his own sex and its value.

Theoretically, according to Freud, the child feels himself to be in competition with the parent of his own sex for the affection of the parent of the opposite sex. Furthermore, according to Freud little girls feel somewhat inferior because they lack the genitals of little boys and little boys tend to fear that unless they assert themselves successfully they may become the "weaker sex."

Ideally, the way out of these dilemmas was to become proud of one's own sex, its social role and function. Again according to Freud, this occurred most auspiciously if the parent of the same sex was kindly, worthy of imitation, and proud of his or her own place in the family.

Specifically, if a little girl's mother is herself more rather than less pleased with being a woman, wife, and mother, the likelihood of her being affectionate and accepting of the little girl is increased. In turn, the little girl comes to respect, admire, and love her mother, and the consequence is a reflected pride in being a female. Similarly, a father who is reasonably comfortable in his role as the benign masculinely assertive figure in the family tends to be both a respect-worthy and nonfearsome object for his son. The son wishes to be a man like his father, is not afraid that his father will resent this equality, and in maturity is effortlessly a male.

As in cross-sex parental relationships, so in feelings toward one's own sex and the parent of one's own sex, there are innumerable variations. We shall try to give the reader a conceptual framework in which to think by making further reference in this new context to the three cases which we have cited earlier in this chapter.

Looking back at Laura's case, we recall that she was well liked by female colleagues and friends and by children. She was sociable with women, seemed not antagonistic toward other teachers, and appeared not threatened in her relationships with mothers of children in her class. We would say that the particular equilibrium Laura achieved in her relationships with both men and women, children, and older people was an outgrowth not only of the pleasantly reciprocal relationships she had with her father but also of the admiration and affection she was able to feel for her mother. Her mother bore no grudge against Laura because of the time spent with the father on his interests. Rather the mother felt herself to be a valued member of the family, doing without indignity the multitudinous chores which are part of the life of a rural housewife. In sum, she was an example of (1) a mother friendly toward her daughter; (2) a mother pleased with her function and life as a woman, wife, and mother and hence not in competition with her husband; (3) a person whom Laura wanted to be, at least in part, like.

The relationship between Ed and his father, like the relationship between Ed and his mother, was somewhat confused and conflicted. The father, unsure of his own role of authority, was more absent than present in family affairs. He was a "good provider" but the cost was long working hours. He was aggressive in his discipline, more often than not in an irritable fashion. He would intervene when the quarrels at home became too strident, contradict the mother's decisions, deny the existence of any difficulty, and, all in all, was as unpredictable as, and certainly less warm toward his son than was the mother. Ed's behavior perhaps becomes more understandable in light of this particular relationship at home. He was defiant, sulky, quarrelsome, unreliable, and erratic. He not only could not form stable relationships with peers of either sex but, when he was not buying their affection with elaborate parties and possessions, he was an isolate. Both teachers and parents warned other children not to play with him. We feel that Ed's lack of knowledge of where he stood in relationship to the role of his own sex and in all interpersonal relations followed psychologically from his father's uncertainty. Ed was ineffectively, inappropriately, and apparently indirectly aggressive as well as coquettish, partially, we feel, as a result of his father's own insecurity as a father. In brief, the parent of the same sex with whom the child ordinarily seeks to be like was, in Ed's case, though not at all cruel, himself a "Will o' the wisp" in the boy's life.

Larry's relationship with his father provides still another variation on the theme of how feelings toward one's own sex develop. Larry's mother was the more active parent in determining child-rearing practices in this home, but Larry's father, a scientist, was by no means uninterested or passive. Although exceedingly preoccupied with his professional activities, he took both pains and pleasure, when Larry was five, in taking the boy to football and baseball games, playing catch with him on occasions, and discussing politics with him. He was, it seemed to us, a father who rather liked being a father and who was proud to have a precocious son. Larry, in his relationships with boys and girls, men and women, seemed uncertain. He was assertive and aggressive intellectually, competitive without assurance, and seemed constantly swinging from cockiness to anxiety and dependency. He treated other children with disdain sometimes, making fun of their "provincial interests" in games or comic books. At other times he hung about groups of either boys or girls, not knowing how to get in. At still other times, when the activity was scholastic, he was confidently class leader. He had no close friendships with members of either sex, and his teachers tended to be uncomfortable around him because of his intellectual demands and sophistication.

We think that Larry's case is illustrative of these points: (1) it is difficult for a child to know what is expected of his sex if the parents themselves are not clear about their own roles; (2) the confusion is increased if one parent "babies" the male child and the other parent inconsistently tries to "make a man out of him"; (3) the confusion is less disastrous if both parents have at least some areas of genuine agreement on child rearing —as in this case the parents' pride in and encouragement of Larry's intellect and brightness; (4) although Larry was by no means sure whether it was better for him to be a boy or a girl, he found that he could make himself distinguished (and thus an individual) by exploitation of his intellectual endowments.

This concludes our discussion of what are for us the three major problems the child faces in his development during the Oedipal period. We reaffirm that these problems do not exist in a social vacuum. As we have pointed out in Chapter 1, adult personality is a consequence of a particular familial setting which is inseparable from the socioeconomic climate of the times and the child's physical heredity. Our contention, however, in this chapter is that between the ages of approximately four and six of greatest significance are: (1) genital sexual activity, for sexual activities may have their genesis at this time; (2) feelings toward the parent of the opposite sex, for nonexploitative and reciprocal affection may lay the basis for similar emotional relationships with members of the opposite sex in maturity; and (3) feelings toward the parent of the same sex, for if the child's same-sex parent is loving, worthy, and at least moderately happy with his social and psychological role, the child has before him a vital example of the satisfactions and gratifications that await him in maturity.

It is too dramatic to say that the die is cast during the first six years of life. Certainly, though, potter's clay is more easily formed during the period when the material is most plastic and is more difficult to change later on. Nevertheless, individuals seem to go on making, as a result of emotionally telling relationships and circumstances, modifications in their attitudes and behavior. Neighbors, peers, teachers, psychiatrists, and psychologists can and do contribute to personality development.

Furthermore, the child at adolescence, as we shall see in the chapters on adolescence, appears to recapitulate the first three phases of psychosexual development. There is thus the opportunity for parents who are wiser emotionally at this time or for the school to help the child to establish better interpersonal relationships and attitudes toward himself.

This ends our description of the Freudian view of what happens during the first six years of life. In order that the theoretical material may take on more meaning for the reader, we shall, in the two succeeding chapters, re-examine the concepts we have already presented, but from a different approach. In Chapter 6 we shall diagram the forces at work during the first six years of life, and in Chapter 7 we shall try to bring them to life by presenting a unified case study of a family of four.

PERSONALITY DEVELOPMENT

DIAGRAMED

In the preceding chapters we have presented, primarily from a Freudian point of view, theoretical concepts of how a child's personality develops. We have discussed the interaction of external forces with innate or libidinal energy at the several significant periods during the first six years.

Although we know of no single method which fully describes the vitality, the fluidity, and the dynamic nature of human personality development, we believe with Kurt Lewin [1] that diagrams sometimes can show interacting *forces* and their movement better than words. In this chapter, therefore, we shall diagram the theory that we have presented in the preceding chapters.

In our diagrams we show the organism always in relation to the total influences of the three major stages of personality development. The three areas (the large circles in our diagrams)

[1] See Kurt Lewin, *Principles of Topological Psychology* (McGraw-Hill, 1936).

should be thought of as representing the three phases of the child's development. Each implicitly represents all the forces and counterforces present during this particular phase of the child's development.

One can see in our diagrams, as in life, that no phase is independent of another but that they overlap and blend together. Furthermore, the three phases are not sharply delineated but are only periods of first blossoming, and each continues to operate in succeeding stages.

What are some of the things our diagrams show? (1) the human organism at birth as a mass of diffuse and undifferentiated potentialities with a force to grow through the first six years; (2) the three phases of psychosexual development and their overlapping so that no one phase is completely isolated from another; and (3) the presence of forces from without which act upon the organism, encouraging some and discouraging other behaviors, thereby contributing to the establishment of basic personality.

We caution the student again and again to view these diagrams as necessarily two-dimensional representations of what is a multidimensional phenomenon. Life at best does not lend itself easily to formulas or graphs. Of necessity, artists and scientists must attempt to capture it through a variety of symbols, visual and auditory imagery, mathematical equations, chemical analyses, and so on. Each of these media contributes to human understanding of the life process, but none in itself is fully adequate for each person, each life, or each student of life. Therefore, the student of life who wishes to understand its processes and development must make use of all of them. Hence the reader should examine our diagrams and captions not only in full context of the theory we have presented but also in relationship to his own life and to the case material which appears throughout this book.

FIGURE I

In Figure I we see the human organism, as represented by the inner circle, in relationship to the three phases of personality development, which are represented by the three large circles. Here also we see within the organism the libidinal, or innate, force to grow, as shown by the arrows within the inner circle, which as yet have no primary direction except the survival of the organism. It is important to note that the three phases of personality development are not superimposed upon the organism but are really extensions of it, for as seen in Figure I they are present, inherent but undifferentiated, within the organism.

It is in this diagram that the reader sees the human organism at birth. Present within the organism is all the potential for the three phases of development. At this time, however, these have no individuality or distinction within the organism, and there is no direction by forces from without. This is the time during which the major effort, on the part of both the organism and the adults who are responsible for it, is directed toward physiological survival. In a sense, this is the brief interlude between the emergence of the organism from the fetus stage and the onset of the process of development and socialization.

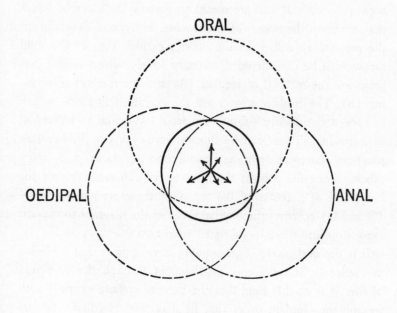

FIGURE I

FIGURE II

In Figure II, changes begin to take place. The inner circle is broken, and never again will the organism be represented as simple and rounded. The libido extends its energy through the break in the direction of differentiating the oral potential of the organism. The reader will note the introduction of a new group of arrows in this diagram. They are seen entering the oral-phase area from without and are meant to portray the external forces that act upon the organism, influencing the type of development the personality will make during this period. Two of the solid arrows can be considered as primary forces, which in this diagram are the method of feeding (A) and the method of weaning (B). The broken arrows are the contributing forces which in type and quantity subtly vary from individual to individual to individual. These can be thought of as current child-rearing practices, parental attitudes, socioeconomic status, and many others. Since the goal at this time is the differentiating of the oral phase of potential of the organism, there are outside forces (C and D) entering the overlap areas of the diagram to prevent expansion into these less differentiated areas.

It is the oral phase of personality development that is shown in Figure II. It represents development through the first year of life. It is at this time that the parents are preoccupied with feeding the child in order that he may live. His first interpersonal relationships become centered around his feeding, and the relationships then are influenced by a multiplicity of factors. As we pointed out in Chapter 3, if the feeding and weaning are strictly scheduled behaviors, the child's first interpersonal relationships will be of one kind and if there is inconsistency in both parental feelings for the child and their feeding and weaning practices, certainly development through this phase will take on a different meaning. Hence in this diagram the reader sees that the amount of orality, the kind of orality, and the meaning of the orality are being developed.

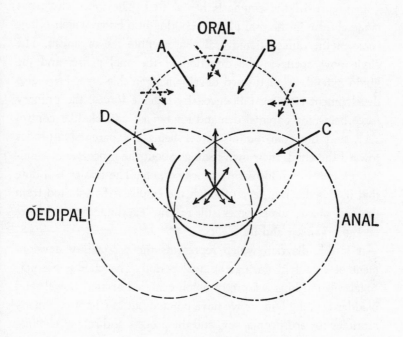

FIGURE II

FIGURE III

In Figure III the emphasis has shifted. The inner circle has made closure in the oral phase, resulting in a bulge which brings some of the differentiated oral phase within the organism. The circle now opens in the direction of the anal phase, and the libido extends itself toward development in this area. Here also development is being influenced by outside forces, the primary force being the parents' demand for bowel- and bladder-control (A), and the contributing forces being the parental attitudes toward the child, their own feelings about the processes of elimination, current child-rearing processes, etc. The reader will note that in this diagram, even though the emphasis has shifted from the oral phase, some forces still remain, exerting some pressure on the organism and its orality.

It is this diagram which represents the personality development of the child during the anal period. The child's interpersonal relationships are pretty much centered around bowel- and bladder-training and, as we have pointed out in Chapter 4, many attitudes toward people, sex, and the process and role of elimination have their beginnings here.

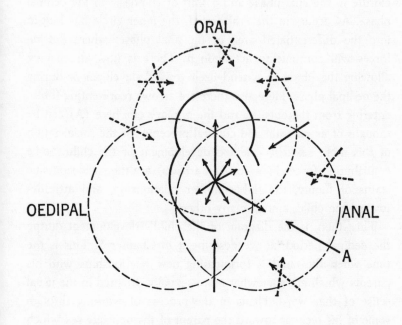

FIGURE III

FIGURE IV

In Figure IV, the process of development has resulted in closure in the anal phase and a shift of emphasis to the oedipal phase. As occurs in the oral period, the inner circle has bulged into the differentiated area of the anal phase, where outside forces will continue to act upon it. There is now an opening allowing the libido to extend itself toward development during the oedipal phase. Here also there are arrows representing forces entering from the outside, and the primary one here (A) can be thought of as parental and cultural precepts for the socialization of this more sexually oriented development of the child. Some contributing forces here (broken arrows) are the socioeconomic status of family, the father-mother relationship, and attitudes toward the child, among many others.

This, then, is the diagram of the child's development during the oedipal period, as we describe it in Chapter 5. This is the time when the child is formulating new relationships with his parents which are somewhat more sexually oriented in the usual sense of that word. He is in the process of working through some of his feelings toward the parent of the opposite sex which will influence his future heterosexual relationships. Furthermore, the development of feelings regarding his own sex through his relationship with the parent of the same sex is a product of this phase of personality growth.

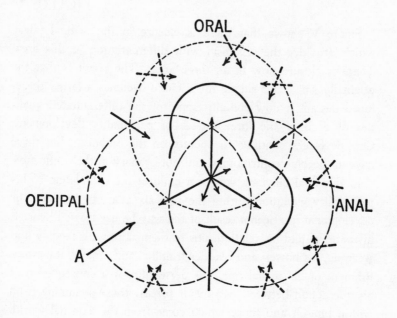

FIGURE IV

FIGURE V

Figure V shows that there is closure in the oedipal phase which provides the organism with differentiation in this area. There is closure now in all three areas. The result is that the originally small and simple inner circle becomes a larger three-lobed design. It now contains some of the differentiated qualities of each of the three phases of personality development. Outside forces continue to operate on the organism, but these have all become contributory and not primary in their influence.

In this final diagram, we see a child at the completion of his personality evolution during the first six years of his life. His development has been a result of the way he has viewed himself, his parents, and his relationships to them during his feeding and weaning, his bowel- and bladder-training, and, finally, the establishment of his sexual role. His personality is a consequence of an interaction between two major forces: those stemming from within himself and those which come from the external world.

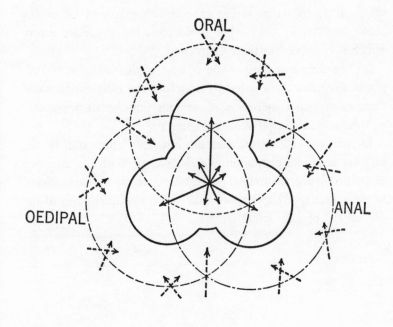

FIGURE V

SUMMARY

In summation of this chapter we want to draw to the reader's attention two main points:

1. These five diagrams show by means of circles and arrows the development of the child during the first six years, which we have described in earlier chapters; they cannot be understood apart from the verbal presentation of Freudian theory which is contained in these chapters.

2. The diagrams portray the process of development according to Freudian theory; by no stretch of the imagination could there exist such a well-rounded, smooth, unindented personality as is hypothetically pictured in Figure V.

In our next chapter we shall illustrate this latter point by describing how real people grow and develop. With the intention of climaxing the theoretical presentation which we have offered in these first six chapters, we shall present a description of the life history of two actual children.

Chapter 7

A CASE STUDY OF
A FAMILY

L IFE is more than a diagram and a theory. Parents and teachers are confronted with real children, and our present intention is to vivify what we have previously stated more formally.

In the first five chapters, we presented some concepts of what goes into the making of personality. In the sixth chapter we diagramed the forces which moved personality, and we depicted these forces as they operate in the formative years. In this chapter we shall describe a family which we know personally, with the objective of illustrating in narrative form what we have discussed in theory.[1] We shall do these things: (1) portray a family of four; (2) show some of the significant influences, both internal and external, upon the family; (3) interpret these data to

---

[1] We are particularly indebted to Robert White, who more methodically tried to analyze the forces molding a personality in *Lives in Progress* (Dryden, 1952), and we are also impressed by John Dos Passos' efforts in his fictional trilogy, *U.S.A.* (Modern Library, 1937), to make sense out of the diversity of forces which go together in making up an individual.

the reader, leaving open the opportunity for further interpretation.

PARENTAL BACKGROUND

We shall call the father Ted and the mother Ann. They both came from substantial middle-class, Middle Western families, and both consciously desired to rear children successfully. For them, "success" meant a pleasant, congenial family in which each member had both rights and responsibilities. They were not at all sure how they were going to accomplish this, but they were sure that they did not want to impose careers on their children; that rearing children was a joint enterprise of mother and father; and that there should be specialists, such as a pediatrician, outside the family who could be called in for advice.

In order to enjoy the freedom which they knew would in part have to be relinquished with the establishment of a family, the parents purposely spent eight years without having children. According to plan, when Ted was 29 and Ann was 28, they conceived their first child. At this time Ted was employed and succeeding as a teacher but was also pursuing his studies in order to increase the earning power of the family and his own professional status. Ann was keeping house. Both consciously looked forward to "the adventure" of being parents but, not unlike many of their friends, they were somewhat worried, annoyed, and uneasy over the "newness" of the project, the "challenge," and the inevitable giving up of being children themselves.

The world did not seem to impinge too significantly upon this family. By this we mean that money was not a problem, because both Ted and Ann had parents to whom they could look for financial help and because Ted had never had trouble in finding or holding an economically comfortable job. True, World War II was imminent, but it was, at the time, something one read about and discussed but with which one did not feel personally involved.

THE ORAL PERIOD

The nine months of pregnancy with Joann were pleasant, being marked by an absence of friction or anxiety on the part of the parents and by good health for Ann. In brief, the prenatal and neonatal atmosphere, physiologically and psychologically, was auspicious. Ann returned from the hospital in a week's time. A pediatrician was employed on a monthly basis, and Ann and Ted set out to rear a child who as an adult would live her life as successfully as possible.

This was a time in the history of child-rearing practices when parents and pediatricians were betwixt and between the opinion that coddling their children by picking them up whenever they cried showed the children that they were loved and the opinion that rigid training, especially in the feeding, was necessary to produce a controlled and self-disciplined adult. Ted, Ann, and the pediatrician tended to swing from such extremes as not picking Joann up when she cried if she were not actually in physical pain and being especially cautious about the hazards of her falling as she began to creep and walk. Although they were restrained in their coddling, they were enormously proud of her. The parents did not force precocious maturation in walking and talking upon her, but they did see that she adhered to the schedule of quality and quantity of feeding which the pediatrician prescribed, no matter how many lost hours of sleep this meant for them at night.

Feeding and weaning were considered by parents of this period as specialties of pediatricians. The four-hour schedule was in vogue, as was the measured formula. If the contemporary reader wonders why the parents, seemingly intelligent people, were overly literal in following the pediatrician's advice, he should remember that in 1940, middle-class parents looked with all good will to child-rearing specialists for authority. In order to do a "good job," they read government pamphlets, which at that time indicated the behaviorist point of view,[2] attended parent-education classes, and consulted regularly with physicians about how and when a child should be fed.

Joann's feeding was marked by rigidity. She was moved within a month after birth to a four-hour feeding routine; the night feeding was eliminated at about this time; the amount she was to eat was prescribed according to her height and weight. All the conditions set up by the pediatrician were strictly adhered to by the parents. Every effort was made to get Joann to eat all she was supposed to eat, at the time she was supposed to eat, even though she had to be burped or glared at. The bottle, propped up by a pillow, was placed in her mouth, and everyone devoutly hoped she would finish it within one half hour. If she cried between meal times and was in good health and not stuck by a safety pin, she was not fed, since "bad habits" and an "overdemanding" attitude might grow from such indulgence.

Weaning also was accomplished in a determined manner. The pediatrician advised that since the child had become accustomed to a bottle and would not like to give it up for a cup, the whole transition might take as long as a day. Consequently as a celebration of Joann's first birthday, she was given a cup to drink from instead of the expected bottle—a gesture which she bitterly but unsuccessfully resented.

The reader should bear in mind that this is not a pathological study; the parents, although ambivalent about being parents and about the burden of parenthood, enjoyed having a child, watch-

[2] Martha Wolfenstein's "Trends in Infant Care," *American Journal of Orthopsychiatry*, Jan. 1953, discusses the influence of child-development theory on child-rearing practices in our culture.

ing her grow, and talking with her, even though they were somewhat inflexible in her feeding schedule.

We hypothesize that up to this time the main forces in Joann's
personality development were: (1) the genuine affection of her
parents for each other and for Joann; (2) some erratic measures
in discipline as the result of her parents' own insecurity about
being parents and of their particular psychology; (3) Joann's
superior endowments in appearance and health; (4) the stability
of the socioeconomic position of the parents during Joann's oral
period; and (5) the fact that Joann was reared by two parents
who had love and respect for her and each other, even though
they made some errors in judgment about child-rearing techniques.

Joann's oral period was superficially in sharp contrast to that
of her brother, Michael, who was born four years later. His first
year of life was marked by a separation in the family because of
the father's induction into the army as well as by the daily
presence of grandparents, who, belonging to an earlier generation, believed that feeding should be accompanied by personal
contact. Michael ate when he was hungry and at the age of two
he had gradually come to prefer drinking from a cup rather than
a bottle.

THE ANAL PERIOD

During Joann's second and third year, the parents met a psychologist and read new books which pointed out that it takes
time and patience for parents to teach bowel- and bladder-control. Joann was taught to use the toilet through leisurely instruction. There were no punishments and no rewards, and there
was no ado when "accidents" occurred. This same attitude was
adopted in the training of Michael. Both children achieved

bowel- and bladder-control by the age of three and never regressed.

In both Michael's and Joann's anal periods (between their ages of two and three) these forces were operating: (1) the parents were not so concerned and anxious as they had been during Joann's oral period; (2) they had greater confidence in their ability to make decisions on their own about discipline and control in general; (3) their increased maturity seemed to enable them to cope with the trauma of family separation because of the war; (4) the problems of sibling rivalry began as a result of Michael's birth. We raise the hypothesis that the acceptance and gradualness of bowel- and bladder-training, accompanied by increased assurance of their role as parents, made for both Joann and Michael an anal period of comparative tranquility. This gave the parents an opportunity to rectify some of the overstrictness and overprecaution which they had exhibited during Joann's oral period.

THE OEDIPAL PERIOD

It was during Joann's fourth year that Ted was drafted; Ann returned to her parents' home in the Middle West; Michael was born. Thus, the expected father-daughter relationship of these years was absent. However, Joann's grandfather took the role of father substitute. Joann also had ample objects for feminine identification in her grandmother, who enjoyed being a housewife, and her own mother, who made special efforts to spend more time with her, take private trips, and discuss the temporariness of the living situation. Ted wrote to Joann directly in an attempt to maintain a contact as a father. Nevertheless, the Oedipal period was not so smooth for Joann as the anal period had been. The world *did* now impinge: World War II made necessary a change in homes, in friends, and in nursery school. Added to these social forces was the inevitable introduction of the "sibling problem," to which we have already referred. The introduction of a brother and the necessity for sharing with him affections which had been entirely her own were somewhat bewildering to Joann. In fact, it was not until early adolescence that she was really able to be on good terms with both her brother and her father. Joann's Oedipal period ended with the reunion of the family at the close of the war when she was elated to return to her own home and familiar surroundings.

Michael's Oedipal period was in sharp contrast to Joann's. Ted was re-established in his profession; the family was again a unit, and the parents' ideas about child rearing had been tried and modified through their experiences with Joann. There was for Michael, therefore, both more stability in one respect and more latitude in another. He missed some of the discipline meted out to Joann but had the benefit of the assured family relationship of father, mother, and sibling. He never knew what it meant to have to give in to usurping younger siblings or to give up a parent overnight.

SUMMARY

These descriptions of the primary events in two children's lives during the first six years have shown some of the things that happened that we think affect personality development. We now contrast the two children as they are six years after the close of Michael's Oedipal period.

Michael is impatient with routines, inclined to be demanding but loving and friendly, self-reliant, and willing to take chances. We would say that the permissiveness during the oral and anal periods, the absence of depriving sibling rivalry and the father's presence during the Oedipal period are the important contributions to this admixture of personality traits.

Joann took some time to gain confidence in her abilities and to secure her inner poise. As she approached adolescence, she ceased being resentful of boys and took pride in her winsome appearance and her capacity to make friends. She came to enjoy learning, although remnants of fearfulness of failure in school were not entirely dispelled. It is our opinion that these traits are causally related to the caution and overdiscipline that were characteristic of her oral period; to the leniency and absence of punitiveness during her anal period; and to both a stable substitute home during the Oedipal period and to the parents' later conscious effort to make up for inevitable lacks during that time. This they attempted to do by helping her work through her sibling problem and creating a close psychological contact between her and her father.

We do not place a value judgment on the adjustment of these children. We have given in narrative form a description of forces that operated on two real individuals during the three phases of psychosexual development.

With this chapter, we conclude our discussion of these developmental years. In the next Part, we turn our attention to the development of the child as he makes his first major break from the home. These are the years when he is of elementary-school age.

PART TWO

The Elementary-School Years

AN INTRODUCTION

THE ELEMENTARY-SCHOOL YEARS are usually thought of as between the ages of five or six and eleven or twelve. They lie psychologically between the Oedipal period and adolescence.[1] The child has, theoretically, resolved the problems of the oral and the anal periods also. He has not yet been faced with the challenges that come with rapid growth in adolescence. Freud therefore termed this developmental phase "the latency period," meaning that earlier problems were quiescent; later problems had not yet arisen.

This does not mean that these years are without developmental influence on a child. We think he faces these psychological tasks: (1) he leaves home to enter school; this means

[1] Anna Freud has devoted a great deal of attention to this period. We recommend her *Psychoanalysis for Teachers and Parents* (Emerson, 1935), her *The Ego and the Mechanisms of Defence* (International Universities, 1946), and her work with Dorothy T. Burlingham, *War and Children* (International Universities, 1943). Her commemorial lecture at Clark University and comments made by Robert Richardson Sears, which are reprinted in the *American Journal of Orthopsychiatry* for July 1951, are also revealing. An entirely different point of view is presented in Arnold Gesell's and Frances Ilg's *The Child from Five to Ten* (Harper, 1946).

that he enters for the first time a world that is not completely parent dominated; (2) as a consequence he begins to make choices and to experiment with friends, interests, and activities; (3) he has a new taste of the relationship that exists between himself and authorities other than the parents (both peer and teacher authorities); (4) he has the opportunity to learn not only the tools (reading, writing, and arithmetic) but also a favorable or unfavorable attitude toward them and the discipline that is sometimes required in the acquisition of skills.

Let us take up our first point. Even though the child may have been in nursery school, entrance to kindergarten or the first grade are high points in "the beginning of real life." He is more on his own. Many of his hours away from home are set by authorities other than his parents. He must button his own buttons; he cannot run home when his feelings are hurt; he must follow a prescribed program and in general make another step away from the protecting womb of home life.

The entrance to formal kindergarten is so common an experience that we are aware of what may be happening psychologically to both the mother and the child. In many senses this is the first major and consciously assimilated step toward solidifying his status as a separate human being. He is more clearly on his own than he has been previously. Especially if he has not been in a full-day nursery school, he soon finds that no matter how kindly and maternal his teacher, she expects him to take more care of himself. There are many symbols of his increasing maturity—walking to school, being responsible for one's time, a less individualized program than in nursery schools, care of one's own money to a certain degree, and so on.[2]

As in any move away from dependence by anyone, the child

---

[2] For a description of what can ordinarily be expected of a child at various age levels during the elementary-school years, see Robert J. Havighurst's *Developmental Tasks and Education* (Longmans, 1950).

has mixed feelings. Although he wants the advantages of independence, he fears that what he gives up may be too costly. This is not the first time or the last time that he will be called upon to reconcile the cost and the gains that come with increasing independence.

Mothers appear not uncommonly also to have some ambivalence about the child's entrance into the regular school. The chances are that she will have looked forward to a decrease in the sometimes relentless demands of the four-year-old. On the other hand, she is also losing something and is being reminded both that time is passing and that outsiders will to some extent eventually replace her as a major figure in the child's life. This ambivalence may account for the sometimes overprotecting and erratic emotionalism of mothers bringing their children to school for the first time. Most schools, like hospitals, have found that *in general* if the mother leaves the child in the care of the teacher, the child is better able to take a step toward adjustment. If she remains and is disturbed, the child's anxieties and ambivalences, which reflect her own, may be more difficult for him to deal with.

To conclude the discussion of our first point, we want to re-emphasize that school entry is an adventurous step in growing up; the child is more independent of parents than previously; he likes, although in some cases is alarmed by, this new responsibility. Similarly his mother is proud of his increased maturity and may be consciously or unconsciously pleased that some of her household burdens are lightened. With a friendly, impersonally personal teacher and a stimulating school program, most children seem to be able to relinquish some of their authority to the teacher. In those cases in which timidity on the child's part persists or the mother seems unable to leave the kindergarten room, perhaps the teacher and the principal need the help of a psychological specialist in working things out to the best advantage of all concerned.

Let us turn now to our second point. Once the child has learned to paddle around, so to speak, in the water of school life, his horizons begin to broaden. His selection of friends is no longer restricted to the immediate neighborhood. He will be found, in the first and second grades particularly, to change friends, almost daily. In the later years he becomes more discriminating according to his own tastes and tends to form gangs and cliques.

His intellectual interests are as varied and eclectic as his taste in friends. The interests are indeed multiple, as anyone who has seen the contents of a nine-year-old's pocket or pocketbook can testify. The list of interests may run from deepsea exploration to astronomy and include bugs, dolls, dramatics, crafts, competitive sports, animals and so on, *ad infinitum*.[3]

The heavily increasing scale of interests has many implications for the elementary-school teacher. On the one hand, he finds it relatively easy to avoid boredom and discipline problems since the curriculum can so readily be enriched by studies of stars, television, prehistoric man, farm life, trains, and even folk dancing. On the other hand, the child's interests are often transitory, and he does not tend to delve deeply into a particular subject. Since he is also proving that he is a person apart from adults, he may even, after once displaying an interest in a topic, be negativistic, recalcitrant, and resistant to the teacher's desire to pursue the study that was begun so eagerly.

This brings us logically to our third point—the authority of outsiders. We shall discuss discipline at greater length in a later chapter but we should note here that children seem not only to grow in a social way but to gain stability if they are subject to reasonable and consistent rules and regulations. A teacher who

[3] Paul Witty has made numerous studies pertaining to children's interests. They are summarized in his *Reading and the Educative Process* (Ginn, 1939).

changes the curriculum daily as children's interests change, who does not help the child see a task through to completion, or who follows all whims of his class is not aiding the child in learning to live in a social world. If he is always at the beck and call of his class's momentary whim, he is as befuddling and anxiety-producing to the children as is the strict, unrelenting, dominating teacher.[4]

Not only does the child have new experiences in balancing his relationships with adult authorities (sometimes comparing unfavorably the teacher with the parents and vice versa) but he also has experiences with peers in this respect. Leadership and followership are experimented with both at school and at home in relation to other children. At home he is not uncommonly confronted with the birth of a brother or sister, which means that he may have to learn to share his parents and at the same time take over some of the care of the young sibling and subordinate some of his own desires. At school he finds some children are "good" bosses or leaders; some make a pretense of being so; some are indomitable; and some are simply bullies and he must learn not to be intimidated by them.

In brief, during these years he runs the gamut of authority relationships which he will face in later life and which are not identical with parental authority. How he assimilates and recognizes the existence of extrafamilial authority is a crucial growth and development experience that proceeds in a special way from kindergarten to the sixth grade.

Our fourth point is inseparable from the three we have already discussed: the elementary-school years provide the time for the child to learn those skills which seem necessary for social

---

[4] See, for discussion of this point of view, Fritz Redl and William Wattenberg, *Mental Hygiene in Teaching* (Harcourt, 1951); Henry Clay Lindgren, *Mental Hygiene in Education* (Holt, 1954); Sigmund Gruber, "The Concept of Task Orientation in the Analysis of Play Behaviour of Children Entering Kindergarten," *American Journal of Orthopsychiatry*, April 1954.

and economic survival in an advanced technological culture. He learns writing, spelling, and arithmetic in order that, having discriminated among his interests, he can pursue some of them more productively, either vocationally or avocationally, in later years. Mastery of the skill subjects prepares the way for this development, for security of many types in the extrafamilial world; and, if they are taught so that they are not chores, these skills may even become an avenue for pleasurable use of leisure time in adult life. Mastery of reading, for example, may be a step in preparing the child eventually to find a satisfying job, may help to decrease any fearsomeness of school that may exist, may contribute toward a feeling of well-being because of the accomplishment, and may indicate to him that there can be fun in books as well as in the movies.

In summarizing this point we want to state, with Fritz Redl,[5] not only that learning the tool subjects is a culturally necessary assignment for children and schools during the elementary-school years but that adequate teaching and learning of these subjects have mental-health benefits. If the child's interests are skillfully employed, and at the same time he learns the satisfaction of digging, delving, and completing "jobs" which are not always exciting, he may develop a positive attitude toward learning and work.

To recapitulate our four points, it is a truism that the child of this age is learning that the world is larger than his home. The peer group and authorities outside the home assume an influence that is very great. Mothers are constantly surprised to find that the child who is obstreperous at home conforms easily at school if the teacher has psychological meaning for him. The child gradually learns about rules and regulations, coming to be able to distinguish between those rules which make life easier and those which simply satisfy somebody's desire to make rules. He

[5] Redl and Wattenberg, *op. cit.*

learns this not only through adult-imposed order but also through the numerous clubs and informal groups which he forms with his peers.

Finally, the elementary-school years are a microcosm of the human life: everything happens that happens later, but on a smaller scale. The conflicts between one's self and one's bosses are there; sexual activity is present; the necessity to choose between the immediate impulse and the long-term goal exists in serious form for the first time; the world begins to emerge in its complexity. All these aspects are present in a more diminished way than they are in adolescence but they are not on so diminutive and parent-dominated a scale as they are in the earlier years.

Since everything is happening during the elementary-school years, they present for the parent and teacher, as well as the child, special problems which may manifest themselves in eating, sleeping, lying, stealing, swearing, and sexual behavior. As these areas are of concern to parents and teachers, we shall review them in the next two chapters.

Chapter 9

SPECIAL PROBLEMS

GETTING CHILDREN to eat, dealing with smoking and stealing, supervising extracurricular entertainment, and regulating sleep are some of the more pressing problems parents and teachers encounter during the elementary-school years.[1] In this chapter we shall discuss some questions which frequently arise in our work with teachers and parents. The reader should keep in mind that our views reflect our experience with teachers and parents as well as the research, and also that throughout we are emphasizing the position that what is important in solving a particular problem is the discovery of the psychological meaning of the observable behavior.

As with sexual activities, it is always necessary to attempt to differentiate expected, developmental, and harmless behavior from behavior that is symptomatic of personality disturbance. It

---

[1] Problems of this period were discussed at a workshop held by the American Orthopsychiatric Association in 1950. Edith Buxbaum's account and point of view of the workshop are available in the *American Journal of Orthopsychiatry*, Jan. 1951. Fritz Redl and David Wineman have contributed important information about severe (though nonpsychotic) disturbances in *Children Who Hate* (Free Press, 1952).

would seem desirable, though it is not always possible, for the parent and teacher to divest these problems of their emotionality. Emotionality may becloud the problem, and its origin may be forgotten in the heat of what has become a battle between the adult and the child.

EATING

The first problem area we shall discuss is eating, since research workers report that this is a matter of considerable interest to many parents.[2] Teachers, too, from our observation, are concerned about how to get children to eat balanced meals in the school cafeteria. One wonders why eating becomes such a problem. In view of the fact that people eat because of biological requirements, the problem seems to us to be more apparent than real. It is probable that underprivileged children for whom food is not easy to come by do not have to be urged to eat. Perhaps in some future time, child psychologists will wonder just what went on in the twentieth century when they learn of the obsession on the part of so many people of the middle class with the eating problem. A lecturer to such groups sometimes comes away with the impression that children at birth are surely resolved to starve themselves to death and are thwarted only by the most valiant efforts of their mothers and teachers.

Many parents point out that, all things being equal, children who have the opportunity to eat a balanced diet seem over a period of time to regulate both the quantity and also the balance of food according to their particular physiological needs. They may go on sprees during which they may eat more heavily or more lightly or concentrate on certain foods. They may be too tired or too stimulated to eat some meals, especially if the meal-

[2] The reader is referred to Arthur T. Jersild, *Child Psychology* (Prentice-Hall, 1954), who presents many researches on eating.

time is accompanied by quarreling or nagging. Parents whose children are pronounced physically fit by a physician have successfully allowed their children freedom of choice and quantity of what is served to the rest of the family and have often found that eating problems disappear.[3]

What sometimes happens, however, is that at mealtimes the child does not eat what is on the table. He may receive threats or promises about dessert. Teachers may warn that no one may leave the lunchroom until all plates are clean. The end results are that both adults and children become irritable and a little war develops in which it would seem that victory is more important to both parties than the eating.

When eating is not made such an issue, children seem to learn (1) to select as much food as they can eat (thereby eliminating conflict over wastefulness); (2) that they are eating for themselves and not for someone else; and (3) that they cannot blackmail their parents into running a restaurant with a menu.

Candy eating and gum chewing seem also to be emotionally highly charged issues. Our experience indicates, however, that often children can wisely regulate their candy consumption. If not deprived, they do not gorge themselves, although at certain ages it seems that their expenditure of energy requires more sugar than at other ages. When there is deprivation, candy eating may become both excessive and compulsive.

What has been said does not apply to the eating habits of children who display signs of emotional disturbance. There can be eating problems which arise from especially emotionally laden situations. A child, for example, who has just been presented with a baby brother or sister may feel he has been dethroned. He is particularly sensitive to the amount of time and care that his mother devotes to feeding the sibling. He may consciously or

[3] See Benjamin Spock, *Pocket Book of Baby and Child Care* (Pocket Books, 1946), pp. 297-346.

unconsciously try to regain his lost position by refusing to eat, by becoming picky about his food, or by overeating. Either under- or overeating not only can be ways of getting back at someone but can also serve to compensate for loss of security. In such cases the parent or teacher may need the help of a specialist in dealing with an eating problem. Scolding or nagging or punishment cannot help because what such a child profoundly wants is a place in the sun and even negative parental behavior gives him this.

A child who is angry or hurt for any reason (*e.g.*, he has been left with an unfriendly baby-sitter; humiliated in front of company; unjustly scolded by a teacher) may resort to non-eating as a weapon. He will continue to do so unless the cause is removed or he is forced to eat.

We are pointing out that the gastric system seems to be one of the most reliable indicators of one's emotional states. Although respiration and circulatory system can signal emotional distress, it is the stomach and one's attitudes toward food (either wanting more or wanting none) that post the signals most quickly. Certainly a child who presents eating problems of any kind should be examined by a physician. If his physical condition seems satisfactory, the parents or teacher should then attempt to evaluate what is going on emotionally, and, if necessary, should enlist psychological or psychiatric aid.

TABLE MANNERS

The topic of table manners often follows a discussion of feeding problems. It has been our experience that often this seems to concern fathers more than mothers. We hypothesize that many fathers reach home still tense from the kind of occupational life middle-class men lead and from commuting. They may be ripe for exploding when the child doesn't use his fork properly. After all, the father has been disciplined all day, and why shouldn't the child be? Nevertheless, it is curious that fathers are so disturbed by manners, since it is part of the folklore that little boys should be messy and dirty and flout the niceties. Possibly the fathers are simply paying back what was done to them.

One difficulty in teaching manners lies in prematurity of the effort to teach them. Adults forget what fine muscular control is necessary if one is to handle a fork and cut properly with a knife. Such controls are not learned in a day. If mealtimes are a time for bickering about table manners when the child does not have adequate neuromuscular coordination, he may become so tense that his table manners become worse.

It may be helpful to parents and teachers to keep in mind that manners are man-made. They are not natural ways of behaving. There is nothing absolute about the way one should hold a fork (the English do it differently). We do not imply that manners should not be taught. In order to live successfully in any society, one must abide by certain of its regulations. We do mean that (unlike walking—a "natural" function) manners need to have meaning to the child. For effective learning, the child needs to have the *why* of good manners explained to him. The why is very simple and understandable: Many people, rightly or wrongly, are offended by poor manners and pleased by good manners, and thus good manners seem to make living with people pleasanter. Therefore, if the child wants to eat at the school cafeteria or at the table with guests, at home or the family, or to go to a restaurant, he must understand that he must use the best manners he is *able* to use.

COURTESY

The problem of manners is not confined solely to those at the table. Learning to say "thank you" and "excuse me" and not being rude are three examples of other kinds of manners. Children appear to be able to learn that people like real friendliness and that friendliness is sometimes expressed by courteous and thoughtful behavior.

Courtesy can be taught and learned in many ways. We suggest that example can be a good teacher. Rude parents or rude teachers can hardly expect the children in their care to be polite; parents and teachers who rail and rant because the children do not write thank-you notes and in the end write the thank-you notes for them are not contributing toward an innate politeness; parents and teachers who either docilely accept rudeness from children or imperturbably and insensibly are rude and superior are setting up a double standard of manners. Conversely, polite, friendly, democratic teachers and parents who have standards and hew to them may be teaching courtesy in the most lasting way.

Regardless of how loved and respected and exemplary the child's parents are, what his peers think carries great weight with him. During the elementary-school years to comb your hair and be clean may be thought "sissy," or to be very polite may be thought to be "apple polishing." "The teacher's pet" is not in an enviable position with his classmates. However, if adults persevere, they will probably find that when the child begins to socialize, at dances and parties during adolescence, he will become unbearably clean and polite, and overly critical of the parents' and teacher's manners.

SLEEPING

Sleeping and eating problems have much in common. Both sleeping and eating are functions that might be termed "natural." Yet in a highly organized society such as ours their naturalness sometimes finds itself in conflict with time requirements, opportunities, and the current preconceptions. In both sleeping and eating there are wide individual differences in the amount and quality which the body requires. This is true for both adults and children. Some children sleep lightly and others deeply. Some benefit greatly from catnaps. In short, as the research indicates, there is a considerable variation here—among individuals and among the several developmental stages.[4] The arbitrary afternoon nap is a case in point. Some children outgrow the need for it before others. It may be true that they don't know when to tone down their activities and that they need adults to make provisions for quiet play, not necessarily sleep. It is also true that sometimes it is the mother who needs the nap time more than the children. Similarly, kindergarten and primary teachers may need a rest as well as their children, but there is no proof that children must pass out on a mat in order to relax.

Generally children will go to sleep when they are tired. Again we must except the child who is trying to gain control over his parents because he consciously or unconsciously knows that his staying awake upsets them. Continued sleep disturbances, including nightmares and insomnia, suggest that all is not well and that outside help may be required.

To return to the child without special problems, getting to sleep may become a temporary problem when he is overstimulated by too much excitement directly before bedtime. For a child who has been to an adult party, or whose home atmosphere is momentarily tense, or whose parents indulge in roughhouse play with him at bedtime, special help in going to sleep is necessary—a quiet story for example.

Fear of the dark is not unusual in children. It sometimes appears now in those who may not have displayed it in their first years of life. It may be related to a greater awareness of the

[4] The periodical *The Nervous Child* devoted its Jan. 1949 issue to articles and reports of researches on sleeping.

physical environment and a growing ability to distinguish between light and dark. Children may be easily aided in overcoming this fear by permitting them to have a small light in their room. The child learns from such an experience that there is really nothing in the dark to fear, and within several years he should be able freely to give up the night light.

Children are like adults in that they may enjoy rituals to help them prepare for sleep. Many adults have bedtime rituals: winding the clock, putting out the cat, brushing their teeth, eating a snack, and so on. In a situation in which one cannot perform his rituals, he may sleep less well.

One of the most common rituals of children is taking a stuffed animal to bed. They remain loyal to the animal long after the stuffing is gone. The animal evidently helps the child to go to sleep and, when the need for it no longer exists, he will give it up. It should always be kept in mind that the healthy person throws away crutches when he has outgrown them. If he does not, it is important to find out why not.

STEALING

Stealing is another behavior of this period that causes anxiety among parents and teachers. As with the other behaviors we have mentioned, stealing by children of elementary-school age needs first to be viewed as a normal part of the developmental process. Boys, especially, at about the age of nine, go through a period of taking from stores things which they don't need. This applies to favorably situated economic groups as well as to those that are underprivileged. We can only speculate as to why. Possibly the boy is asserting that he is growing up and that he can defy those whom until now he has looked up to. This is a gang age. In their new-found independence, children group together both for security and for the excitement of defying parents and teachers who up until now have been the "bosses."

Stealing, which is outlawed in our culture, may be a manifestation of gang assertiveness, and it is a rare child who can isolate himself from the mores of his peer group. Hence, stealing does not necessarily mean that the child will become a professional burglar. Threats and overpunishment are often not only useless but may drive the child to cleverer concealment or make him unduly fearful and submissive to parental authority.

There are very sound social reasons for not stealing which, if they are stripped of emotion, the child can readily accept. In our experience, children understand the reason that you cannot lock everything up all the time yourself and it would be unpleasant to live in a world in which you had to. Children even find amusement which may lead to the cessation of stealing if they are told about the Dobuans,[5] who live in a culture in which one can never trust anyone else. Sometimes it is helpful for the child to hear his father or principal tell of his own exploits as a child, discussing the commonness of and the reasons for such behavior. Such a discussion may conclude with a joint working through between the adult and child as to how to make restitution of the stolen property.

Economic background cannot, however, be disregarded. Some stealing goes on because children are placed in a situation in which they must steal or lose face because they don't have the money to spend that other children have. Schools have a special obligation in this respect. A school that has candy sales, entertainments, and other events which pupils must pay for has an obligation to see that underprivileged children have some opportunity to earn money for them. We might mention in passing that

[5] The Dobuans illustrate very dramatically the interrelationship between culture and personality. Their way of life is reported in Ruth Benedict's *Patterns of Culture* (Houghton Mifflin, 1934), Chap. 5.

teachers need to keep their own money away from children so as not to supply temptation.

It can be seen that the causes for stealing at this age may be of several varieties: gang pressures, defiances, negativism as a way of establishing one's individuality and independence, or economic status. There may also be subtler reasons for stealing—reasons with Freudian connotations. A boy may steal in order to prove his manliness, or a girl may steal because she wishes conciously or unconsciously to show that she is as strong and aggressive as a boy. A child of either sex may steal because (unconsciously) collecting material things is a way of establishing that he or she is worthy and in possession of the situation. (This is not unlike the accumulation by some adults of worldly goods at the expense of everything else.)

In summary, stealing falls generally into two categories: it may be part of the normal process of growing up, or it may be evidence of a possibly serious emotional problem. In neither case does retaliatory punishment appear to be permanently effective, and when stealing is repetitive, we feel that a specialist's help may be needed in dealing with the problem.

SMOKING

Problems arising out of smoking are not very different from those relating to stealing. Both smoking and stealing seem to symbolize to the child that he is growing up. Children have for ages indulged in activities pursued by adults but forbidden by them. As often as not, it seems likely that many children during the elementary-school years smoke temporarily for experimental reasons. It is our opinion that some schools and homes actually motivate the child to more smoking by overemphasizing his feeling that he is tasting forbidden fruits.

Often children smoke to show that they are growing up; to

see what it feels like; to do what their parents do; or to defy overrestrictive adult control. If the adults make an issue of smoking, it may become more of a titillating experiment for the child. If, as in stealing, the adult attempts to divest the problem of emotionality, and if he is not punitive, the habit may tend to disappear.

One adult behavior seems to contribute to continuance of these "bad habits." We refer to the confusion that appears to occur in children's minds when they are arbitrarily forbidden practices that are openly engaged in by parents and teachers. A child is reproved for lying and a few minutes later hears his mother tell the neighbors a falsehood. Fathers may swear but not their sons. Adults may boast about their successful income-tax evasion or getting out of paying a parking fine, but they become enraged if their children steal apples from a neighbor's tree. Until adults can follow the standards they set up for their children, it is probable that the children will imitate what they do rather than listen to what they say.

We conclude our discussion of smoking by emphasizing once again that any behavior during the elementary-school years which appears in exaggerated form may be symptomatic of a possibly serious emotional disturbance. If the parent or teacher suspects this to be the case, the aid of a specialist should be enlisted.

COMIC BOOKS, RADIO, MOVIES, AND TELEVISION

Parents and teachers often worry about the influence of comic books, radio, and movies. Although the research is inconclusive as to whether the effects of these media are harmful or beneficial, we can make assumptions on the basis of general psychological propositions.

Wertham [6] emphasizes that disturbed children may act out fantasies which are stimulated by comic books. Homicide and jumping off roofs may in some cases have been stimulated by what has been read or seen. Similarly, children not mature enough, whether because of chronological age or mental retardation, to distinguish between reality and fantasy may try to live out this kind of literature. In our opinion, therefore, undoubtedly some children are harmfully stimulated by some of these media. These children need guidance and supervision, and sometimes their problems should be brought to the attention of specialists.

It is our observation, however, that many children normally pass through, without harm to themselves, phases of intense interest in radio or television adventures and movies or comic books which are not approved by their elders. If afforded an interest in other kinds of entertainment, such as better literature, they eventually become bored with the repetitiousness of the mediocre. On the other hand, if parents and teachers make an issue of the matter and fail to show that fantasies can be satisfied in other kinds of esthetic experiences, even the "normal" child may not outgrow his reliance on the pornographic, the sadistic, or the sentimental.

Many if not most children become satiated with the lurid if parents and teachers do not create an interest in it by prohibitions. We might add that most children and other people read and look at what is vicariously exciting as a way of relieving daily stresses. It is our guess that there will always be western movies, mystery stories, soap operas, science fiction, and light romantic fiction, and that there will be people who will find release and enjoyment in them.

Parents and teachers may accept this formulation but genuinely fear that the child may become fixated at this level of

[6] See Fredric Wertham, *Seduction of the Innocent* (Rinehart, 1954).

fantasy and never know the gratifications that come from other kinds of reading or drama. Banning does not seem to be the way out, as children seem clever enough to get past the bans. We once taught a group of children from faculty homes, where comic reading was a sin, and we were always stumbling across children from such homes hiding in a cabinet reading a comic book. Comic books lost some of their fascination when they were permitted in the classroom after all tasks had been completed. Furthermore, in some cases, comic books, radio, television, and movies proved to be stimuli for wider reading, as when adventure stories or books which have contributed to motion pictures were brought into the classroom.

SUMMARY

We have made these points in this chapter:

1. The elementary-school years are those during which the child experiments with and expresses his new-found independence in ways that often place him in a position of conflict with adults.

2. The areas of particular conflict seem to be in behaviors involving eating, sleeping, manners, smoking, stealing, swearing, lying, and choice of commercial entertainment.

3. Basic to these conflicts seems to be an adult-defying attitude, but for us this attitude is not unexpected in a child who is making forays toward the establishment of his own identity and who is exploring the world.

4. Ordinarily, these behaviors do not become destructive if the parent or teacher allows a reasonable degree of latitude, discusses with the child why certain behaviors are not permissible, and at times disciplines consistently but without retaliatory emotion.

5. If, however, the behaviors or conflict situations persist or become exaggerated, they may be symptomatic of individual emotional disturbances, which are met best with the help of a specialist.

The reader will note that we have not touched upon children's sexual activities at this age. They exist, of course, and so many questions are asked about them by parents and teachers that the next chapter is devoted exclusively to this topic.

Chapter 10

THE PROBLEM OF SEX

~~~~~~

IN THIS chapter we are documenting a position supported by research—that children have genital sexual interests during the elementary-school years and that these interests are "normal." [1] It was not too long ago that children who evinced interest in their bodies or who asked questions about them were considered by adults to be "oversexed." Little did the parents know, for example, that most if not all of the parents in the neighborhood were also regarding their child as unique in this respect.

We now have, however, not only daily observation but considerable statistical material from Kinsey as well as reports of other research workers that this interest is infinitely more common than uncommon. The kindergartener goes through a period of "playing doctor"—taking rectal temperatures. He asks where babies come from and how and why the sexes differ. He engages in genital manipulation (masturbation). Just as children of the

---

[1] See Alfred C. Kinsey *et al., Sexual Behavior in the Human Male* (Saunders, 1948), Chap. 5; Benjamin Spock, *Pocket Book of Baby and Child Care* (Pocket Books, 1946) pp. 299-305; Clellan S. Ford and Frank A. Beach, *Patterns of Sexual Behaviour* (Harper, 1951), Chap. 13.

elementary-school age are curious about many things, so are they about sex and their sexual feelings. Some of the activities of this period which often disturb parents and teachers include sex questions and sexual play of all types, including voyeurism (peeping for pleasure) and the use of "dirty" words.

The problem for the teacher and the parent is not simple in relation to these matters. The adult has some educative obligation to help children see how their activities must be curtailed in view of social customs. It is also important to know that sometimes these behaviors in specific children are not a phase of normal development but are symptomatic and indicative of emotional disturbance and if ignored or improperly treated may result in the deepening of the disturbance.

It is not surprising that adults are genuinely distressed by children's sexual activities. As usual, with problems which have emotional content, things get mixed up and reversed. Popular attitudes toward masturbation, for example, have gone through various evolutionary phases. Around the turn of the century, masturbation was thought to be a cause of serious illness, particularly of mental illness. This folk belief still prevails among certain sections of the population. One occasionally runs across a parent who uses the most drastic methods of punishment, sincerely believing that otherwise the child will be intellectually damaged. Psychoses (severe mental illnesses) were also at one time thought to be traceable to masturbation. Perhaps the incidence of *dementia praecox* (a particular form of severe mental illness) during adolescence and the high incidence of masturbation at this period may have been one reason. Perhaps this example helps the reader to see how easy it was for this false causal relationship to have been made.

In the 1920's, however, medical opinion became quite conclusive that masturbation caused neither intellectual deterioration nor schizophrenia (a synonym for dementia praecox). Still it was vaguely considered a bad thing, which perhaps, if excessive, would lead to general weakness and to withdrawal from social contacts. Visiting counselors to high schools expressed the prevailing opinion to boys (to the latter's amusement and shock) that "99 percent of the boys 'did it' and the hundreth was a liar," but the boys were advised to keep the "habit" in check. This was the period when cold baths and vigorous physical exercise were considered as preventive measures against excessive masturbation.

The great fear was that masturbation could become habitual and that the boy (or girl) would never seek "normal" sexual outlets. Actually, in determining whether or not a behavior will be perpetuated, the degree and accessibility of gratification are far more important than mere repetition. Unless there are psychological or environmental reasons which prevent an individual from relating to other people, it seems usual for adults eventually to find greater satisfaction in a sexual act with another person.

But to return to the evolutional development of popular attitudes toward masturbation, since about 1940 there has been one point on which the psychological and the medical profession have been in almost complete agreement: that is, that masturbation *per se* is not necessarily physically or psychologically damaging. It may be a behavior which recurs in different stages of development and is not harmful or it may be a symptom of emotional disturbance. It is the latter with which we are now concerned.

Teachers and parents understandably ask when masturbation ceases to be a phase of development and becomes symptomatic of emotional disturbance. The answer cannot be given in terms of quantity or even in terms of what is "appropriate" at any given age. "Too much" becomes too much if the behavior curtails and interferes with other relationships.

To speak more concretely, a child of ten who frequently locks himself in his room and masturbates when other children are out playing may be exhibiting symptomatic behavior. On the other hand, he may be simply physically more mature and closer to puberty than most of his age group and the behavior may be normal for him. The only way that normal and symptomatic activity can be distinguished from each other is in context of the whole personality. If the child who locks himself in his room also retreats from social contact or tends to retreat from the usual play, and if there are other signs of lack of confidence in peer relationship, then his masturbatory activities may be considered symptomatic.

The significance of the distinction between normal and symptomatic behavior is that its treatment differs. In "normal" masturbation, the teacher and parent would probably ignore the whole matter. If a child with indications of emotional disturbance masturbates, the activity should not be so lightly dismissed. The chances are that the child is guilt-ridden about his sexual feelings and that masturbation complicates this guilt. With such cases, the help of the specialist who can work with cases of personality disturbances may be needed by parents and teacher.

What we have said about masturbation applies in general to other sexual activities during the elementary-school years. Voyeurism at this age, for example, may be an expression of normal curiosity. The five-year-old who has become aware of the physical differences between the sexes may want to see for himself what these differences are. From the ages of 9 to about 11, the child may be curious not only about differences but about sex relationships and may search out opportunities to watch. Again, unless the personality shows signs of disturbances, voyeurism can be viewed as the only way in which the child can find out what he wants to know.

Sexual interests are manifested not only in watching what people do but also in watching animal sexual play and reading presumably "naughty" books. In some homes the family "doctor book" with its charts of the human anatomy used to be locked up by the parents only to be ferreted out by the child when they were away. Although some literature that children find is frankly pornographic, much that they consider titillating is actually innocent. It seems to us likely that in homes and schools in which the library and dictionary are totally accessible, some of the guilt-producing forbidden delights of reading about sex would diminish.

The use of "dirty" words by children, whether profane or obscene, is often a matter of great concern to adults. Children first use "dirty" words around the ages of four or five, when they are building a vocabulary and pick up any words. They are delighted to find that they have stumbled upon certain words that cause surprising reactions in adults. Often they are confused because the parents will alternately laugh and scold them when they say these words. As they grow older, children use such words almost as a badge to show that they are growing up. They are imitating their big brothers and sisters and parents. These also may be words used by the gang, and their use symbolizes membership in this in-group.

Such use of "dirty" words, which includes writing on the sidewalk and on toilet walls, is to be expected, especially if one considers that there is sometimes sexual excitement and defiance involved in drawing and labeling crude pictures. The motivation of defiance may decrease if the child knows that his parents and teachers are familiar with these "secretive" words and are not shocked by them. It is important for him to learn that he is more socially acceptable if he knows the appropriate place for the appropriate behavior: fingers at picnics, forks at the dinner table.

But, again, the child who is obsessed by profanity or obscenity and who demonstrates general uneasiness with himself may be exhibiting symptomatic behavior. He may be unable to work through and consolidate his sexual drives at that point, or he may be compelled either by the environment or by internal conditions to act in an aggressive and hostile manner toward adults. In either case the cause must be sought if treatment is to be effective.

Since children's sexual activities have often been upsetting and puzzling to parents and teachers, these activities have not infrequently been seen as problems. At one period in the nineteenth century, adults attempted to deny that sexual interest existed at all during the elementary-school years. At another historical period, any observed sexual behavior was sternly punished. At still another time, children were diverted by adults from sexual activity.

Around 1930, the whole problem of sex education became a matter of preoccupation for adults concerned with children's growth and development. The principal objective of sex education has remained fairly constant: guidance of psychosexual development in order that sexuality become divested of guilt, confusion, misunderstanding, and fearfulness during childhood.

The methods of educating, however, have changed. Today most specialists believe that imparting of the "facts" of sexual anatomy and physiology resolves little of the child's uneasiness. They believe that a child can be overexposed (his questions answered in too great detail; too much made of frankness). The view today seems to be this: (1) the facts are important but the feelings of the adult who informs the child of the "facts" are what are crucial; (2) sex education, like any other education, must take into account the readiness of the child to assimilate understandings and details; (3) sex education cannot occur in a vacuum; its effectiveness is dependent upon cultural, community, and familial values and attitudes and interrelationships. In brief, it is part of the whole constellation of the child's education, and the direction it takes (whether in school, at home, or in various children's organizations; whether with the aid of books or films or not) can be determined only by taking into consideration all these factors and by consultations among all who are concerned.

In summary, we want to leave with the reader these points:

1. Whereas, according to Freudian theory, sexual or erogenous interests of the child during his first five years were focused either around particular nongenital zones or, if genitally oriented, the main object of feeling was one's self or a member of one's family, during the elementary-school years, children's sexual activities take on distinctive characteristics: (*a*) they are genitally oriented and directed toward peers and extrafamilial individuals; (*b*) although they have a genuine sensual meaning, these activities are often transitory, intermittent, and subordinate to other interests; (*c*) they bear the earmarks of general curiosity and exploration of the unfolding new world as well as having sexual connotations.

2. During these years sexual activities may have diverse psychological meanings, none of them necessarily pathological: (*a*) a child may be finding himself and establishing the separateness by the age-old device of rebelling or defying what is prescribed by those who have dominated him up to now; (*b*) he may, on the other hand, be so disturbed in his relations with adults and his peers and so ill at ease with his growing freedom that his sexual activities may become all absorbing and symptomatic rather than part of the "normal" growth phases we maintain they usually are.

3. Sex education by home and school may help the child to pass through these years of experimentation with a minimum of discomfort, but if his interests seem to be obsessive or compulsive, the help of a specialist may be indicated.

PART THREE

Adolescence

Chapter 11

A DESCRIPTION

Aᴅᴏʟᴇꜱᴄᴇɴᴄᴇ is often a period in life which is marked by enormous variability and complexity. Part of the difficulty in categorizing and analyzing this period (except in general terms) is that its boundaries shift, depending upon the criteria used for its definition.[1] Some authorities regard adolescence as beginning with physiological maturation; sociologically it terminates when he legally comes of age at anywhere from 18 to 21 chronological years. We are reminded by economists that its duration may vary with the family income—*i.e.*, if his family is poor, the adolescent may set up his own home earlier than if his family is well off and can financially provide for him longer. Some psychologists say that in one sense of the word adolescence may last throughout an

[1] The reader will find voluminous references on adolescence in any library catalogue. We select the following for his consideration: the classic work, G. Stanley Hall, *Adolescence*, 2 vols. (D. Appleton and Co., 1925); the psychoanalytic case studies in Peter Blos, *The Adolescent Personality* (Appleton-Century-Crofts, 1941); the practical and readable descriptions of individual adolescents in John W. M. Rothney, *The High School Student* (Dryden, 1953); the sociological study, A. B. Hollingshead, *Elmtown's Youth* (Wiley, 1949); the statistical and factual survey, Robert J. Havighurst and Hilda Taba, *Adolescent Character and Personality* (Wiley, 1949).

individual's life—*i.e.*, some individuals seem to be unable to act independently and maturely no matter how old they get. And even meteorology must be considered, for we know that climate may play a not indecisive role—*i.e.*, the physiological changes which are part and parcel of adolescence appear to be influenced by climatic conditions.

Adolescence was investigated around the turn of the century by G. Stanley Hall. Some of Hall's findings, published in his pioneering work, *The Adolescent*, have stood the scrutiny of further study but on one major issue contemporary opinion is divergent. Until about the middle of the 1920's, it was commonly believed by students of adolescence that, because of the effect of the biological changes within the teen-ager, this period was inevitably one of storm and stress. It therefore came as quite a surprise to some when Margaret Mead, an anthropologist, reported that in Samoa adolescence was the period when life was enjoyed most intensely. She found that childhood in Samoa was a very restricted period because of the many demands imposed by one's elders and that adulthood was burdensome because of the responsibilities of maintaining life and family. By contrast, adolescence (the in-between period) was free and idyllic. An adolescent fished because he wanted to fish; sex was not considered shameful; and adults encouraged in adolescents the active pursuit of happiness.

Since Mead's contribution, we have had numerous other studies which show that adolescence does not have the same psychological meaning in all cultures.[2] These studies offer reason-

[2] Anthropology has contributed a variety of studies. From these, we have chosen Margaret Mead, *Coming of Age in Samoa* (Modern Library, 1928), and Clyde K. Kluckhohn and Dorothea Cross Leighton, *Children of the People* (Harvard, 1937); those collected in Douglas C. Haring (ed.), *Personal Character and Cultural Milieu* (Syracuse, 1948), especially those papers by Mary E. Johnson, Gregory Bateson and Frances W. Underwood, and Irma Honigman; and finally Cora Dubois, *People of the Alors* (Minneapolis, 1944).

ably conclusive evidence that adolescence is not necessarily pleasant and problem-free or unpleasant and problem-loaded. Its nature is determined by the specific interaction between the culture and human biology.

Adolescence is by no means idyllic in all primitive cultures, but by making comparative studies of primitive and nonprimitive cultures we are able to analyze some of the reasons for the presence or absence of stress. Four psychological characteristics seem to stand out in those cultures in which adolescence is less of a trial than it is so often in our own:

1. the adolescent knows what is expected of him;

2. he is not alone in making the transition to adulthood;

3. the period itself does not extend so far beyond the time of physiological maturity as it does with us;

4. its terminus is clearly defined.

In such cultures the adolescent may be subjected to various thoroughly distasteful, painful, and actually humiliating tests which he must pass before he is granted the status of being grown up. He may be buried temporarily in an anthill or be forced to run up a hill without spilling the water from a container which he is carrying on his head. But the tasks are clearly defined; he is assured of the standards for grading him; and he knows that if he passes them he will succeed in attaining the status of adulthood as it is defined by that particular culture.

This is a quite different situation from the changing and often capricious expectations for the adolescent in our culture. One night he is told he must act responsibly "because he is grown up now" and the next night he is denied the use of the family car "because he isn't old enough."

Another difference is that the adolescent in cultures more favorable to this period knows when adolescence is over. When he is graduated to adulthood, his new status is clear to him as well as to other adults. In our own culture a veteran of World

War II, if he attends a dormitory college, may be told when to go to bed until he receives his bachelor's degree.

Next, since the adolescent in a primitive culture may be assumed to be a man or woman earlier than in our own, he is permitted sexual intercourse earlier, and thus the strain of expected abstinence, which plays such a powerful role in adolescence in our culture, is reduced. In brief, the granting of adulthood in primitive cultures seems more closely related to physiological maturity.

Lastly, under optimal cultural conditions, the adolescent passes through this period with a group-awareness. He will not be the only individual riding upside-down on a wild horse. Others may be undergoing the same test at the same time, or, at the very least, he knows that they will or that they have. In our culture, adolescents seek to band together in cliques, but these are informal, often of a transitory nature, and structured by the adolescents themselves out of their bewilderment.

In some primitive cultures adolescents know not only what is expected of them during this period but also by tradition are formed into bands or groups for exchange of information. By contrast, in Western culture, adolescents not only are expected to be grown-ups one day and children the next but they are further handicapped by individual isolation, which is broken through fortuitously and often secretively. Although there are innumerable youth groups which promote social activities among teen-agers, in our experience we have been constantly confronted with the quest of the adolescent for a group in which he can talk freely about matters many of which seem to be considered unmentionable by his elders: nocturnal emissions; how it feels to menstruate; God; sexual feelings in general; and so on. Some adolescents do form cliques and groups, sometimes defiant of their elders (secret fraternities in high school), often small and often informal, in which these issues are talked about.

Our point is that the structured and guided organization of adolescents which facilitates the intercommunication and exchange of feelings seems more prevalent in primitive cultures in which adolescence is less strenuous than in ours.

In all cultures, it goes without saying, adolescence has in common characteristic physiological changes, but, as we have said, these do not necessarily produce conflict. The term for this physiological beginning of adolescence is "puberty," which means simply the onset of rapid growth toward adult physical status and bodily changes which enable the human organism to reproduce the species.

Puberty does not begin during the same year of life for all individuals, and the physiological changes do not occur in the same sequence for each individual. We have become increasingly aware that signals of approaching puberty occur before the actual beginning of puberty, and a number of psychologists have become interested in the prepubescent period. Signs of on-coming puberty may be observed in girls as young as eight or nine, and in rare cases even earlier. In boys, the onset is somewhat later, perhaps in the tenth year. The average age of puberty in girls is about twelve and in boys about thirteen. On the other hand, late maturers are not uncommon and some individuals of either sex do not become physically mature until fifteen or sixteen or in some cases even later.

In girls, pubescence is marked not only by increasing rate of growth in general but by a filling out of the breasts, a rounding of the hips, and the appearance of body hair around the genitalia and under the arms. The girl assumes a more womanly physique. The occurrence of the first menstrual period (the menarche) indicates that the girl is biologically mature in the sense that she can bear children. The menarche, however, may be succeeded as well as preceded by the secondary physiological changes that we have just mentioned. Moreover, the menarche may not be followed by regular menstrual periods. In some females there is great irregularity in the frequency, physical distress, and quantity of menstrual flow.[3]

In boys, puberty is marked by a rapid increase in stature, the growth of body hair on the legs, around the genitalia, under the arms, and on the face, a deepening of the voice, and an increase in the size of the genitals. The boy's ability to procreate is not marked so clearly and so dramatically as it is in girls. Many boys have nocturnal emissions of semen, which indicate the physiological ability to fertilize the female, but the internal production of spermatozoa is not always announced by the nocturnal emission.

Let us now note a few general points about some of the conflicts or quasi-conflicts of adolescence which are of a psychological nature. If adolescence is defined as a period during which one gives up many of the dependent needs which characterize childhood, it must be understood that it is a period which for a variety of reasons may be prolonged to a considerable extent.

Economic realities, for example, may tend to prolong the psychological dependencies. This is especially true of middle-class families, in which the children are urged to go on for a college education. For the children of such families, financial support in some form, even if only board and room, must often be provided by the parents until graduation. When an individual is being supported, he may feel dependent and obligated to adhere to the requirements and codes of those who support him. Such feelings may produce conflict between wanting to be taken care of, which may have pleasurable aspects, and wanting to be the self-sustaining adult that one is physically and intellectually capable of being.

---

[3] A detailed description of physical changes during puberty is available in Wayne Dennis, "The Adolescent," in Leonard Carmichael (ed.), *Manual of Child Psychology* (Wiley, 1946).

Along with socioeconomic conditions, the emotional relationship of the child to the parent may determine the duration of adolescence. It seems to us perfectly possible for a young person to receive partial or even complete financial aid from his family and achieve a maturity in his interrelations with them. It is also perfectly possible for a young man or a young woman to be economically independent of the parents—indeed, to be a member of a family of his own—and yet be emotionally dependent upon mother and father. However, emotional independence from childhood bonds on one's parents seems to require: (1) the parents' capacity to give up their domination of their children and (2) the child's capacity to become an adult, standing alongside his parents, and not in need of their overprotection in the crises of daily living.[4]

In summary, we can redefine adolescence as the period between childlike dependence upon parents and the establishment of the individual as an interdependent rather than as a dependent or independent human being. It is an age characterized by:

1. rapid physical growth and marked increase in and preoccupation with sexual feelings;

2. confusion over these feelings which is increased in our culture because of restrictions necessarily imposed as a result of the socioeconomic structure;

3. conflicts, in a sense synthetic, which grow out of both the lengthening of the period which occurs inevitably in a complex technological society and special psychological relationships which exist between parent and child. The latter may be a consequence of fewer children in the home, later childbearing on the part of the parents, and increased longevity.

In the next two chapters we shall examine some of the ramifications of these points.

[4] For a discussion of the meaning of maturity, we refer the reader to Erik Erikson, *Childhood and Society* (Norton, 1950).

Chapter 12

SPECIAL PROBLEMS

Adolescence, like the elementary-school period, presents the child and those around him with problems peculiar to the age. These grow out of the interaction among psychosexual development, the sociological environment, and physiological changes. In this chapter we shall interpret the effects of this interaction and examine the resulting special problems.

IDENTITY AND RAPID GROWTH

In a sense, the biggest psychological problem the adolescent faces is that of determining who he is and, more distantly, who he ultimately will be. As Josselyn has written,[1] the adolescent, in contrast with the elementary-school child, almost overnight finds himself with a body which is new and no longer familiar. The rapidity of growth thus has undermined one of the primary sources of the concept of self. Moreover, even if there were no

[1] Irene Josselyn, "The Ego in Adolescence," *American Journal of Orthopsychiatry*, April 1954.

outward bodily changes, the internal and glandular develop-
ments are of such a nature as to produce a set of almost entirely
new sensations. To compound matters, confidence in the body
is reduced because the body is less manageable. The voice and
the limbs are not so controllable as they once were. Awkward-
ness and clumsiness appear erratically, and have long been
sources of humor about this developmental period. The adolescent seems strange to himself and wonders who he is.

Yet the direction of growth, both as result of internal and
external forces, is toward the establishment of identity: by this,
we mean the realization that one is oneself and not another.
His sudden confrontation with ways of feeling and behaving that
are unfamiliar to him presents the adolescent, in some cases
starkly, with the question of just what his identity is. In his
quest to discover the kind of person that exists in his new and
changing body, the adolescent consciously and unconsciously
conducts many experiments in social adaptation. Out of these
experiments in social adaptation, both intra- and interpersonal,
results a concept of self which plays a large role in the self concept of adulthood.

IDENTITY AND SOCIAL ADAPTATION

In the adaptive efforts, the adolescent may become startlingly
different in personality, almost overnight. The studious child in
the elementary school may become a frivolous social butterfly in
high school. The child scholastically uninterested in elementary
school may find many satisfactions in science in high school.
Such apparently irrational changes may represent the search of
the youngster for adaptation most compatible with his own
personality needs and with the culture and subculture in which
he must live. Thus, the teen-ager will experiment with various

ways of adjustment and select the one that seems most satisfactory to him.

It goes without saying that there is no one ideal and universal adaptation. Finding the "right" adaptation for an individual, therefore, becomes a matter of trial and error. Parents and teachers of the adolescent know well from their own observations how capricious are the moods, fads, and interests of this age group. We feel this phenomenon is in part related to the exploration and experimentation that we have just described.

Social adaptation in our culture necessarily has a sexual component. Whereas, during the elementary-school years, sexual curiosity and feeling were both transitory and immediately sensual, during adolescence the problems of what it means to be a man or woman arise.

This seeking for sexual identity aggravates again the Oedipal situation, which, the reader will recall, first appears between the ages of four and six.[2] Early in adolescence the parent of the opposite sex assumes greater importance than was true during the years between six and puberty. Other older adults of the opposite sex also become objects of libidinal drives. Literature and folklore are replete with stories of the adolescent who has a crush upon the teacher of the opposite sex. And, of course, there are strong same-sex ties, since, as we have said one of the ways of resolving the Oedipus is identification with the same-sex parent. Hence boys hero-worship older boys, stronger boys, or the coach, and freshman girls adore senior girls, popular girls, or an able female English teacher.

The new Oedipus situation cannot be maintained, since true reciprocity in the sense the adolescent wishes it (quasi-marriage) is generally impossible. Ordinarily the adolescent turns for companionship and love objects to his peers and contemporaries.

[2] See Oliver S. English and G. H. J. Pearson, *Emotional Problems of Living* (Norton, 1945), Chaps. 3, 10, and 11.

IDENTITY AND REBELLION

Like other developmental phases, adolescence may have violent aspects. In his effort to create his unique personality, the adolescent may sometimes exhibit strange and defiant behavior. A girl, for example, although reared in a mutually loving home, unconsciously wanting to separate herself from the family, may at times, apparently irrationally, flout those standards which she has been reared to live up to and which she has hitherto accepted. The boy from such a home who has always enjoyed being a good student, may choose rebellion against school work for a time as the only way of saying "I am I." This type of behavior is not so different from the negativism of the two- and three-year-old who is distinguishing himself from others by saying "no" even when he would like to say "yes."

As the adolescent becomes convinced that he is a person in his own right, he will likely readopt, although in a modified form, the values and standards of his family group.[3] Many adolescents, however, go through an evolutionary period: "good" little boys or girls become "bad" boys or girls during adolescence and later on turn into pillars of virtue. Agnostic and atheist adolescents are commonly found in ministers' families, but they may later become faithful churchgoers. Rebellion seems to be a part of one's growing up, but generally this kind of rebelliousness tends to disappear once identity is established. Rebellion during adolescence is a manifestation of the need to prove to oneself and to others that one is himself and not a possession or a dependent.

[3] The conflict that goes on in establishing one's identity is clearly evident in numerous fictional works. We remind the reader of such diverse characters as Pierre in Tolstoy's *War and Peace*, the four girls in Louisa May Alcott's *Little Women*, Lymie Peters in William Maxwell's *The Folded Leaf*, and, finally, Alice, in Lewis Carroll's *Alice in Wonderland*, who several times was puzzled as to just who she was.

IDENTITY, DEPENDENCE, AND INDEPENDENCE

The problem area we have just discussed touches upon and overlaps with other problem areas. It is closely related to the dramatic struggle between the desire to be independent and the desire to be taken care of. This struggle appears and reappears through life. We have mentioned it in connection with the child's entrance to school, and it is not absent during the remainder of the elementary-school years. Each party in an engagement faces it, and it does not vanish with marriage. Even in old age there seems to be no escape from this struggle.

The essential difficulty, which may or may not be culturally determined, is evidently the fear that if one allows himself to be cared for he loses his sense of separateness and independence. Conversely, one fears that if one asserts his independence or his individuality, it must be at the cost of seeking care and comfort in any circumstances. Although there may be some validity in assuming a dichotomy between dependence and independence, between separation and unity, the antagonism between the two may be exaggerated. Perhaps the mature individual is neither totally independent nor totally dependent but is interdependent. We think that it is possible for the wife to take care of the whole family in some situations without the husband's losing his sense of self-esteem, and for the husband to be the provider without his wife's feeling enslaved and indebted. Interdependence of this nature, in our opinion, is psychologically possible in all human interpersonal relationships, be they those between parents and children, teachers and students, friends, etc.

Perhaps part of the capriciousness of adolescent behavior is traceable to the violent swing between wanting to be dependent and wanting to be independent. At one moment he may be defiant and at the next may burst into tears or exhibit some other behavior that indicates that he wants to be nurtured. One insightful adolescent whom we knew, after a successful and parent-approved adventure in self-reliance, unaccountably at bedtime could not stop weeping. She finally explained that she didn't want to grow up because then who would take care of her? Another adolescent verbalized similar feelings to her parents, who were relaxed and trusting toward her. She felt that other parents were showing by their concern that they still wanted responsibility for safeguarding their offspring. The inference here is that defiance by adolescent children is not always an assertion of their right to be themselves. At times they are asking their parents to step in and reassert their authority for security purposes.

Often the adolescent seeks a way out of this conflict of dependence versus independence by maintaining his independence from adults while building dependent ties upon his peers. Groups, cliques, or clubs seem long to have been a way for human beings of any age above four or five to banish loneliness and fear, and they serve especially vital purposes during adolescence.[4] It is almost as if children of this age band together in packs because of the frightening consequence of being alone and outside.

VOCATIONAL CHOICE

A thorny question for many adolescents, their parents, and their teachers is that of vocational future. This question seems to be particularly troubling in an advanced technological culture such as our own.[5] Such a culture offers jobs (at the top of its

[4] Phyllis Blanchard touches upon this and other psychological problems in "Adolescent Experience" in J. McV. Hunt, *Personality and the Behaviour Disorders* (Ronald, 1944), Vol. 2.

[5] This problem is dealt with in a substantial manner in Robert S. Lynd and Helen M. Lynd, *Middletown* (Harcourt, 1929). Although this work was published many years ago, much of what it has to say is as valid today as when it was written.

hierarchy) which necessitate specialized and long-term training or education. To fulfill the requirements for them the adolescent must make his vocational choice before he knows who he is and what he wants. He must study subjects which often have only the remotest meaning for him—Latin, if he is to become a doctor; advanced mathematics, if he is to become an engineer; etc. There are more than a few children in college-preparatory courses because of social and parental pressures but with no interest in them. Conversely, there are children with professional potentialities in terminal high school programs because neither they nor their parents can see that college may have a value for them later on.

Both discipline and drop-out problems in the high school sometimes may be related to the fact that the culture, adolescent psychology, and the secondary-school curriculum are not always in accord. Friction at home may arise because the parents "see" the future but do not see the many factors which contribute to the adolescent's confusion in this area.

Educators and psychologists are exploring solutions to the complex oblems of preparing for a vocation before one knows what one wants and is fitted to do. The tendency seems to be in the direction of extending secondary education two years (the junior-college years) during which time the adolescent, being closer to maturity, can better explore the occupations that are appealing and available to him.

ADOLESCENT SEXUALITY

No discussion of the problem areas of adolescence would be complete without mention of the adolescent's sexual needs and impulses. These are years during which the drive toward sexual intercourse, whether of a homosexual or heterosexual nature, becomes imperative in the male, according to Kinsey.[6] In the female, Kinsey has found, the drive for sexual union is more diffused and less compelling but curiosity about sex and sensual interest in sex are nevertheless present.

The culture, both for religious and economic reasons, frowns upon sexual intercourse in this age group. Marriage is not feasible because, under nonemergency conditions, jobs are not open to the adolescent. Premarital intercourse is often thought hazardous by the adolescent because of his ignorance of the act; his fears about illegitimate pregnancy or venereal disease; and because of the girl's conflict between wanting to be "popular" (which she not infrequently interprets as resulting from "heavy petting") and wanting to follow the moral precepts of her parents.

The confusion of adolescence in our culture seems to us almost entirely represented in the sexual area. The "who am I" question to which we have referred before appears in crystallized form: most adolescent males, for example, with powerful biological urges cannot marry because they themselves suspect that such a course would be unsafe for them in their psychological instability—they do not want to settle down or be tied down before they know what kind of futures they want.

On the other hand, not only is the biological impulse imposing but, in both males and females, acting against the sexual mores of their elders can be both a way of rebelling and attempting to establish identity and a way of saying, "I am no longer a child." The "gang" is often no help in solving this problem: males swap stories in a competitive manner about their sexual prowess, not without the purveying of misinformation and confusion to one another. Females exchange stories about "good" and "bad" girls; some may feel called upon to emulate "sexy"

[6] See Alfred C. Kinsey *et al.*, *Sexual Behavior in the Human Male* (Saunders, 1948), Chaps. 5 and 9.

movie stars without having assimilated their own sexual emotions.

Further to complicate the picture, neither sex has a clear picture of what is expected by the opposite sex. Girls are not sure whether they should be tough, sweet, shy, or reticent. Boys have before them stereotypes of hard-boiledness, which rules out any natural gentleness, or of suavity and Don Juan gallantry. Such uncertainty about expectations may make for fumblingness or for compulsive sexual promiscuity and may be a prelude to disillusionment with sex during later years. Lastly, sexual behavior of the adolescent is involved with his prolonged and perhaps gratifying psychological dependence upon his parents. Although he rebels, be he male or female, conscience, identification with parental standards, doubts as to the wisdom of the rebellion, distaste with himself, or the mere fact rebellion against those who take care of him may make for more anxiety in the sexual area.

The problem of adolescent sexuality is, like the problem of vocational choice, one which still awaits solution. All outlets for the release of biological tension, whether through heterosexual intercourse, homosexual intercourse, or masturbation, are socially denied the adolescent. The denial may come from the adolescent himself for the reasons we have already given and hence be psychological also. What is important is that a strong biological urge is counteracted externally or internally in our culture for a longer and longer period of time. (Pioneers could marry at 16 years of age.) The adolescent himself seems well aware of the dilemma in which nature and society have placed him, as is witnessed by his questions directed toward adults whom he can trust and by his efforts to find substitutes in precocious smoking, fast car driving, and drinking. The answer to the question that has appeared at the present time most satisfactory to educators and psychologists has included: a provision during the high-school years for group discussion and the airing of questions by the adolescent in an organized fashion; the opportunity to gain and exchange authentic information; guidance by specialists in sublimation of sexual energy and substitution of objects for satis-fying the sexual drive if abstinence is required; guidance by specialists in increasing the adolescent's understanding of how to fit his sexual drives and sexual outlets into his own psycho-logical and sociological environment: an interpretation of the meaning of masturbation, homosexuality, and heterosexuality for each individual.

SUMMARY

In this chapter our objective has been to interpret what goes on inside the adolescent so that the adult will see him as not just bumptious, boorish, or unpleasant out of willfulness. We pointed out that his main concerns are: to know what to do with his "new" body; to find out who he is and what kind of person he wants to be; to reconcile his own psychological uncertainties with social requirements; to make up his mind about a job; to reconcile his sexual needs and develop his social needs; to estab-lish himself as a separate or rather unique individual, who is still an interdependent member of a family group.

We are not unaware that the world does not revolve around the adolescent. He lives with parents and teachers, and they have feelings too. Hence, we are devoting our next chapter to the adult and the adolescent, with the emphasis upon the adult's side of this interpersonal relationship.

Chapter 13

INTERACTIONS WITH

ADULTS

IN THIS CHAPTER we shall examine the point of view that parents and teachers may react to the adolescent in a particular way because of their own psychology.

This, of course, is a truism in human relations. When two or more people get together, the outcome depends largely upon the action of each personality upon the other. This psychological circumstance raises particularly acute problems during adolescence, since the teen-ager is fast approaching adulthood and the parent or teacher is himself uncertain about his changing status in relation to the adolescents in his charge.

We have found that some adults are burdened by injunctions from within or without themselves that they must always be "scientific," aloof, and judicious. They somehow feel that they are not permitted any moments of irrationality, open irritation, or traces of immaturity. Such a burdensome level of aspiration has seemed to us to produce unnecessary tension and in fact the very "evil" it is intended to avoid: erratic emotional swings, or overly felt distaste or hostility. We have learned that it is sometimes helpful, therefore, to talk with these adults about some of the problems which they face and to try to give them some perspective about them.

These have been some of the matters of concern to teachers and parents of adolescents: (1) feelings about their own age; (2) ambivalence about a decrease of authority and the establishment of a new authority relationship on the part of the adult which differs somewhat from that which existed during the elementary-school years; and (3) reactions to adolescent negativism and the depreciation which seemed to be implied in this negativism.

It has struck us that it may be psychologically significant that parents, especially those of adolescents, are both pleased and somewhat resentful that their children are growing up.[1] It is not entirely far-fetched to presume that some parents with children of fifteen who are as big as they are may be painfully reminded that they themselves are growing older. Our culture seems to place high value on being young, and the increased stature of the adolescent may be a constant reminder that the parent is no longer as young as he used to be. If one has children of five or six, who are much smaller than one's self, one can convincingly claim to be quite youthful, but if one's child towers above one, this becomes more difficult. The result of this inevitable awareness of aging on the adult's part may be effortful and embarrassing attempts to be unseemingly youthful. Fathers sometimes discomfit their adolescent sons and daughters by trying too hard to be "one of the boys" with either their daughter's or their son's friends. When teachers try too hard to be youthful,

---

[1] Some of our hypotheses are discussed in the *American Journal of Orthopsychiatry*, Oct. 1954. Further support for our contentions is to be found in case reports of psychotherapists—*e.g.*, Josie Hilgard, "Sibling Rivalry and Social Heredity," *Psychiatry*, Nov. 1951.

they seem to be heading for trouble, sometimes even becoming objects of contempt for their pupils.

The end product of the adult's forced attempt to be youthful not infrequently appears to be the production of hostility on the part of the youth. The adolescent may remark, "You would have died if you could have seen how she acted at her age," or "I could have died," or "Honestly, I could have just killed my mother [or father] when she [or he] was acting so silly."

It is one thing for an adolescent to act "silly" but evidently quite a different thing for his parents or teachers to lose their dignity. We do not mean to exclude participation by either teacher or parent in adolescent activities if the motivation on the part of the adult arises from enjoyment rather than from an effort to compensate for lost youth. But the adult can be comradely, funny, or informal without loss of dignity and adult status. The adult who tries to be the adolescent's peer may meet rebuffs and rejection from the adolescent. It sometimes happens that a rebuffed "good Joe" teacher or parent retaliates by thinking of the adolescent as being lazy, uninterested in school, disrespectful, or unresponsive.

It is our experience that the adolescent is most respectful and companionable with the adult who "acts his age." Neither pomposity nor coy juvenility appears to make for discipline or harmony in home or school. The parent or teacher who has found gratification in the work and play that are appropriate to his age seems to avoid more naturally both these pitfalls.

The second major point we are making is that some adult-adolescent conflict may derive from the adult's reluctance to recognize that he is not such a powerful authority figure as he once was. Parents of younger children and teachers in the elementary grades can relatively easily control and intimidate this age group, either by strength of personality, threats, or violence. This kind of control has less and less effect on the adolescent.

There may be thus an apparent loss of authority, and this loss may present a considerable challenge to the adult. Teachers and parents may wonder how to exercise control, be fearful because they cannot control adolescents as they can control younger children, or may consciously or unconsciously wish for the "good old days" when they reigned supreme. On the one hand, they may be glad that they have less responsibilty than they would have with elementary-school children but, on the other hand, both uncertainty and imminent dethronement which accompanies increased self-direction in adolescence can be unsettling to adults. If the adult feels no loss of face with the increased equalitarianism of the adolescent, he may comfortably and stably maintain his authority role. Cajoling, hollow threats, and other immature attempts to discipline should be kept at a minimum. The adolescent wants authority, as we have said, but not from a person who "throws his weight around" because he cannot accept the relinquishment of his absolutism.

For all these reasons the age of adolescence may be threatening to some adults who have previously been the unchallenged authorities. Our contention is that adults who have not needed to base their self-esteem on control of children are less likely to be disturbed by adolescence than those adults who gain emotional security by "bossing." In our experience, the adult who has some satisfaction both in his work and with his peers is less inclined to be disturbed because the adolescent is no longer a child. Such an adult does not experience a feeling of competition from the adolescent as the latter becomes capable of making decisions of his own. This seems true even when the adolescent displays talent that exceeds that of the teacher or has less need for dependence upon the parents.

Our third point is that if parents or teachers are themselves able to accept both middle age and the resulting new relationship with the younger generation, they handle with more equanimity and more stability the minor manifestations of negativism and rebellion which seem to characterize adolescence. They make fewer scenes over temporary and ephemeral "ill chosen friendships," food preferences (dill pickles preferred to carrots), speech mannerisms, and adoration of other adults. They accept without distress their children's experimentations in literature, politics, religion, and entertainment and are able to recollect their own teen-age years of experimentation. This is not to say that the negativism of adolescence is absorbed docilely by the parents or teacher. Few people like "freshness," rudeness, or disregard of their own feelings. However, under the psychological conditions we have described, we feel the parent or teacher is able to deal, both more effectively and with less stress, with the negativism of adolescence.

For a variety of reasons, negativism sometimes goes beyond the ordinary trial-and-error of self-assertion. There are adolescents who are "delinquent," destructive in their behavior to themselves and others, and overly bewildered. These adolescents present special problems in their relationships with adults, and studies of the best way to help them resolve the problems should be made by specialists.

In summary, we say that if the adult has found some satisfaction in being an adult and in adult relationships, he can provide the guidance and the authority which the adolescent wishes from him. Adolescents have told us that they want in their parents or teachers neither siblings nor dictators. They want authorities who have come to terms with their own lives, who are able both to exercise and relinquish control, and who *can* discipline but who do not *have* to discipline. One adolescent summed up this position when he said he wanted his parents to sit down with him and talk out problems of values and authority; he also wanted his parents to assert themselves on certain occasions while remembering that all people sometimes learn best from mildly unhappy mistakes.

But what we have been saying essentially in this chapter is that this kind of relationship between the adolescent and adult is more likely to occur if the adult understands and resolves some of his own ambivalences about being an adult. The point has been basically simple: the teacher or parent who likes being grown up, who does not have to yearn for the "good old days," and who finds satisfactions in each new age earns respect and friendship of the adolescent. Discipline problems may thus be reduced and guidance becomes of the quality which is a necessity for this age of bewilderment.

PART FOUR

Educational Psychology

Chapter 14

A PREVIEW

W ITH Chapter 13 we completed our discussion of how the human personality develops from birth through adolescence. We now call the reader's attention to the problem which daily concerns the teacher: How do children learn? Perhaps no other matter except that of discipline (classroom control and organization) so preoccupies both the inexperienced and experienced teacher. Hour by hour during the school day he is confronted with questions of how to teach everything from manners to mathematics, and it is small wonder that he asks his college instructor and supervisor for practical help in this aspect of teaching.

Learning in the classroom rests upon three interrelated pillars: (1) theories of learning; (2) general application of these theories to the classroom (educational psychology); (3) specific methods of applying these theories instructionally.Our plan in this section is to bring together some of the prevailing concepts in these areas. In this chapter we shall discuss learning theory and principles of educational psychology. In the following several chapters we shall elaborate our ideas on such special problems as motivation, maturation, intelligence, and evaluation, which we consider especially pertinent to educational psychology.

Gates and his associates present this definition of learning: "Learning is the modification of behavior through experience and training." [1] The term "learning" is easier to define than the process of learning. Many significant contributions have been made to the understanding of how learning takes place, but it must be stated that for the classroom teacher there is some justification in J. Paul Leonard's remark, "Without doubt much of the great confusion in education today is due to the even greater confusion in psychology. We need a more acceptable and convincing explanation of human learning and behavior." [2]

Yet despite contradictions and an absence of full agreement in learning theory, a critical examination of the contributions of learning theorists may provide clues and useful hypotheses for the teacher.[3] The question-answer method of Socrates may still be a way of stimulating thinking and learning at all ages. The logical rules formulated by Aristotle cannot be disregarded in teaching the student how to reason and avoid fallacy. Similarly, Dewey's five steps in thinking, which begin with the accumulation of facts and the setting of the problem and conclude with the solution may play a role in all learning. Even the medieval insistence that learning came about through repetitious copying may be used to advantage in the classroom. Furthermore, the ideas voiced by John Locke and by Rousseau that one learns out of direct experience can be utilized in the classroom. Ebbinghaus cannot be ignored when the problem of why and how one forgets and remembers is under consideration. Thorndike's laws of use, disuse, effect, and connections are

[1] See Arthur I. Gates, *et al.*, *Educational Psychology* (Macmillan, 1948).
[2] See J. Paul Leonard, *Developing the Secondary School Curriculum* (Rinehart, rev. ed. 1953).
[3] See Ernest R. Hilgard, *Theories of Learning* (Appleton-Century-Crofts, 1948).

valuable attempts to synthesize previous thinking about learning. We conclude this kaleidoscopic picture of historical contributions to learning theory by reference to the neurological approach of the conditioned reflex of Pavlov which became part of the behaviorists' approach to education; to the Gestaltist concept that learning occurs when parts are seen in relation to the whole; and finally to the thinking of Kurt Lewin, who contended that one must consider not only relationships but also goals, barriers, and motivations.

These ideas have been translated from learning theory into practice in numerous books on educational psychology.[4] Educational psychology is concerned with the study and presentation of the principles of learning: the role of the will in learning; development of the desire to learn; the relationship between growth and readiness to learn; intelligence, etc. Educational psychology is further refined and its principles are more precisely applied by the specialists in educational methods. Brueckner, for example, integrates learning theory and educational psychology when he writes on how to teach arithmetic;[5] McCullough and Strang perform the same service when they offer the teacher help in the teaching of reading;[6] Hockett does the same thing for all elementary-school subjects.[7]

It can be seen that adequate preparation for teaching includes thorough study of learning theory, educational psychology, and methods of teaching. This, of course, is the standard curriculum for the teacher in training. It would be impossible for any single book, or course, to do full justice to all of these topics. We shall attempt, though, to summarize very briefly the important find-

[4] See Gates *et al., op. cit.*
[5] Leo J. Brueckner, *Making Arithmetic Meaningful* (John C. Winston, 1953).
[6] C. McCullough and R. Strang, *Problems in the Improvement of Reading* (McGraw-Hill, 1946).
[7] John A. Hockett and E. W. Jacobsen, *Modern Practices in the Elementary School* (Ginn, 1938).

ings of learning theorists, educational psychologists, and method specialists in the following statements:

1. *Children seem to learn best when there are gratifying results (pleasures or usefulness) for them.* In other words, when one sees and enjoys results from his endeavors, he tends to endeavor more.

2. *Children seem to learn with more facility and economy when they use and find useful what they are being taught.* Any subject seems learned best if the teacher can find a use for it in the child's life or can even create a synthetic environment in the schoolroom in which the subject can be put to use.

3. *Repetition and drill on certain types of materials to be learned seem to be necessary for many children in the acquisition of information.* However, if the repetition and the drill are not accompanied by some kind of satisfaction and purpose, forgetting occurs out of proportion to the energy expended by the teacher and the child on the task. In brief, the multiplication tables are seldom learned in a day simply by going over and over them. They must be learned not only by repetition but by variation of activity and by making them in some way meaningful.

4. *Children learn best at the point of psychological and physical growth which is most favorable for assimilation of the material to be learned.* High-school Latin for example is most economically taught and learned when the mental age, motivation and stimuli, and background information of the student coincide into a state of readiness.

5. *Native intellectual ability is a factor in learning.* It determines in part what can be taught, how it can be taught, and at what rate it can be taught.

6. *Many children seem to learn effectively when they understand relations of parts to wholes and when they see the Gestalt (pattern) of what they are being taught.* Thus, teaching history

in units, for example, may make a battle or war more memorable and intelligible to the child; teaching subtraction as the logical obverse of addition may make arithmetical reasoning more intelligible.

Some of these principles of learning are stated differently and some new ones are included in a list prepared by the National Education Association: [8]

1. Growth and development are continuous.

2. Behavior is learned.

3. Learning and growth are stimulated by both security and adventure.

4. Each individual is unique.

5. We learn what we live.

6. We always learn several different things at the same time.

7. We learn a great deal and learn it rather permanently by example.

We have in this chapter abstracted historically and from current sources what we consider the essential principles of learning theory and educational psychology. Moreover, these abstractions refer to concrete classroom situations which either a college student or the teacher in service can illustrate in his own learning. Motivation, understanding of relationships, discipline in memorization, and excitement in investigation of new ideas are not restricted to children. Perhaps the best way for a teacher to know how a child learns and what the principles of educational psychology mean is to recall the time and ways he learned most effectively.

But, in conclusion, and before we begin a more detailed examination of learning we want to emphasize that even though the teacher may learn about learning from an analysis of his own education, no two people are the same or learn the same amount

[8] See the Educational Policies Commission, *Education for All American Children* (National Education Association, 1948).

in the same way. An effective teacher seems to us to be able to translate his life learning experiences into use in the unique classroom situation in which he finds himself, remembering always that there are individual differences and that learning (even under the most ideal conditions) does not occur at an even, smooth, continually forward pace. There are peaks, valleys, and plateaus in classroom learning just as there are in any other kind.

Chapter 15

MOTIVATION

<hr>

ONE OF the key problems in both learning and teaching, and hence in educational psychology and methods of instruction, is that of inducing and utilizing the "will to learn." The will to learn we term *motivation*. Without motivation, learning is ephemeral at best; and the more profound and deep the motivation, the more lasting and assimilated and acted upon is the learning. Motivation can arise from felt needs of the child but such needs can, and sometimes necessarily must, be initially prepared by the teacher. Finally, motivation cannot exist in a vacuum: the best motivation can fail to reach fruition if teaching methods are so ineffectual that they dull it or prove to be overwhelming barriers to it.

Let us first make clear that motivation is significant in all phases of life. The quality and quantity of both work and play are related to the reasons for working and playing. Need, satisfaction, and gratification with results are all factors in motivation. These can arise from many sources, such as fear of not succeeding, pleasure in approbation, or the agreeableness of success.

There are so many sources of motivation that no list can be inclusive. In order that our discussion will be of practical use to the classroom teacher, we shall limit it to an examination of what we call *intrinsic* and *extrinsic* motivations for school learning and the relationship between these two. We define intrinsic motivations for learning in the classroom as those which arise from the satisfying fulfillment of needs felt by the child. We define extrinsic motivations as those which arise from satisfying needs which the child has imposed upon him by the teacher.

To translate these definitions into classroom practice, we offer these examples: (1) a subject is learned as a consequence of intrinsic motivation when a child recognizes either the pleasure or the usefulness of the end product of the learning; (2) a child learns from extrinsic motivations when he feels he "ought" to because of demands made on him by adults or peers or because of a usefulness which he is told will result from his learning.

The line of demarcation between intrinsic and extrinsic motivation is not always clear, and a relationship exists between the two. Ideally, in school situations children learn physics because of the excitement they find in the learning. They learn to read "better" because of the exhilaration they derive from the materials they are reading. However, these motivations are not always available or apparent to the child. The first-grader sees primarily the drudgery in reading primers. Daily exercises which may lead eventually to acquisition of a foreign language and its pleasurable use can quickly become boring to the high-school student.

In a situation which has been developed by adults for children —and which is, therefore, usually felt more important by the adult than by the child—the problem of the teacher, then, is to find extrinsic motivations which sustain the child's interest and will to learn and which satisfy a creative need.

We contend that extrinsic motivations must be used in schools because not all learning situations are such that the child would choose them of his own accord. Many boys at the age of nine would rather be wandering alone by a creek than studying spelling, and many girls of fifteen would rather be at the movies than in a high-school study hall. Yet the school seems to be able to become intrinsically rewarding if certain extrinsic motivations are created by the teacher. Conversely, some extrinsic motivations do not seem to us to yield the results (lasting learning) toward which the school purports to aim.

Let us look at some of the extrinsic motivations first. The traditional ones, of course, are rewards and punishments. In college one studies and "learns" because one needs 120 units for a bachelor's degree and thirty more for a master's degree. Just to make sure that one learns, one also has to accumulate what is considered the necessary number of grade points.

Extrinsic motivation by the use of marks begins almost with the beginning of formal education. From the primary grades to the Ph.D., a student is pushed or controlled or enticed into learning what is "good" for him to learn by the promise of A's or the threat of F's. Examinations are used as weapons to induce learning as often as they are a means of helping the teacher discover where the deficiencies lie and hence how to correct them. The final-examination period in any college and the daily examination period in any lower school is a time of great tension and cramming. Once these pressures no longer exist, however, it is sad to note how few people continue to study, to explore intellectually, and to read. Such extrinsic motivations do not necessarily lead to the intrinsic motivations of pleasure and use of learning.

Grades, examinations, and report cards can have motivational value in learning. Moreover, they can have real values in themselves. They can be helpful for both parent and child in estimating how adequately the child is achieving. They can be helpful to the teacher in assessing how well he is teaching each particular child (as indicated by the child's test scores). But grades, examinations, and report cards, can not be considered as permanent motivations for learning. If the teacher wants the student to learn, it is incumbent upon him to give him some feeling for the value of the subject being taught: to create motivations that are more than skin deep.

There are many ways of doing this. Some subjects, if properly taught, are innately pleasurable and exciting. *Macbeth* can be enjoyable. Logic can be more challenging than any jigsaw puzzle. Science can open up a world. Music, art, and physical education can be sources of delight. Teachers might look for ways to start their teaching with fun, whether it be in playing games in physical education; reading an exciting story in English literature; singing popular songs in music; or bull-sessioning about world affairs in a college political-science course.

If pleasure in a subject is first found by the student, the skillful teacher can the more easily lead him toward memorizing, digging, and outside reading, which otherwise he would do only because of outside pressures.

There are innumerable extrinsic motivations which can be converted by the skillful teacher into stronger and more lasting intrinsic motivations. We cite these examples: Children first want to read because their parents do; the adolescent wants to play the piano because his popular friends do and he wants to be popular; the high-school sophomore wants to learn a foreign language because saying a few foreign words makes him feel superior. But in any of these subjects, the student, as he becomes more able, may carry on the learning because of his recognition of the subject's deeper value for him.

Usefulness is a motivating force that cannot be underestimated. If one can use (intellectually or otherwise) what he learns, he probably will learn it better. Here lies the manifold meaning of Dewey's phrase "to learn by doing."[1] If one can do something with what he learns, one is more eager to learn it; and at the same time the doing helps one to learn. This is another way of saying that effective teaching relates subject matter to actuality wherever possible. But since, as we have said, not all school subjects can be carried on in out-of-school life situations at the time they are being taught, educators have been exploring the possibilities of the "activity program" as a way of teaching.

"Activity" is a term that is confusing to many people. Some parents and teachers feel that an activity program means that children must hammer, saw, throw clay around the room, and make a great deal of noise. By activity program we mean simply student participation in what he is learning. If he is learning arithmetic, he may be playing store. If he is studying prehistoric animals, he may be discussing why evolution took place. He is not just talked at. He may listen to a lecture, but the lecturer makes the subject matter come alive in such a way that the student is actively in his mind reacting to what is being said. He is not just taking notes. Activity may be quiet or noisy, intellectual or muscular, or both, but it is not passively receptive. It means action, interaction, and use, even if not voiced, and it is a way of creating an intrinsic learning situation in an otherwise artificial setting.

Our primary concern in this chapter has been to demonstrate:

[1] Out of John Dewey's many writings, we select as most meaningful for the teacher and parent *Experience and Education* (Macmillan, 1938). See also Caroline Pratt, *I Learn from Children* (Simon & Schuster, 1948).

1. that the will and need to learn is basic to learning;

2. that the more deeply imbedded is this will in the individual, the more lasting will be the learning;

3. that superficial motivations may be necessary to induce deeper motivations;

4. that effective teaching does not remain at the superficial level of motivation but seeks in various ways to bring about more lasting learning.

Chapter 16

MATURATION

WHAT APPEARS to have been one of the most useful discoveries about learning in the last fifty years is the principle of maturation.[1] This principle, which is of exceptional value to teachers, can be stated as follows: *A human being learns most effectively and most easily when he is mature enough (physically, emotionally, and intellectually) to assimilate the material he is supposed to learn.*

Maturation is the process by which the child reaches the point of his growth and development at which he is "ready," from the total point of view, to learn what the teacher wishes to teach him. It is at this point that teaching can be done most

---

[1] The subject of readiness, or maturation, is discussed in many books. For a review of research we again suggest Arthur T. Jersild, *Child Psychology* (Prentice-Hall, 1954). For application of principles to the classroom, see *Fostering Mental Health in Our Schools* (National Education Association, 1950). For a special theoretical discussion of maturation, see the introductory chapter of Arnold Gesell and Frances Ilg, *Infant and Child in the Culture of Today* (Harper, 1943). For description of "age norms" see the latter book, the same authors' *The Child from Five to Ten* (Harper, 1946) and *How Children Develop* (Ohio State University, 1949), a cooperative effort of the staff at this institution.

economically and efficiently for both the child and the teacher.

In its simplest form the necessity for adequate maturity and appropriate readiness is not difficult to understand. Infants are not expected to walk before they have physically developed to the point where they can. To force learning before appropriate maturity has been attained can be either wasteful or detrimental.

Gesell has presented a wealth of documentation on this point, as have other research workers. We ourselves have suggested that to teach manners prematurely or to bowel- and bladder-train before the act is intelligible to the child and the sphincter muscles are under control by the nervous system is uneconomical. The acquisition of motor skills is influenced by the growth and development of the neuromuscular system. Jersild reports various studies which demonstrate that such motor skills as buttoning buttons, cutting with scissors, and climbing stairs can be learned more quickly and taught more easily when the child has achieved physical, intellectual, and emotional readiness and maturity than when attempted before these conditions exist.[2]

The principle of maturation is so apparent in everyday life that the application of it sometimes is oversimplified. To help the teacher understand its application and ramifications, we shall discuss it in relationship to the teaching of reading. What we shall say about learning to read can be applied, however, to learning to walk and talk or to studying psychology.

Let us begin with the assumption that learning to read is not a simple operation. First, to learn to read, the child must be physiologically and anatomically mature enough for this particular learning—*i.e.*, the development of his visual and auditory system cannot be that of an infant, who is unable to discriminate sights and sounds. Moreover, socially and emotionally he should have reached the stage in his growth at which he has the need for and can derive satisfaction from this particular learning.

[2] Jersild, *op. cit.*

True, if these conditions are not present, he can be forced to learn, but there may be too great a cost in time, in the distaste that may develop for reading, and in the energy expended by the teacher. Reading specialists tell us that the average child is intellectually, emotionally, and physically ready to read at the age of six. To try to teach him before is not efficient.

However, there are several exceptions to this proposition. Some children are mature enough and therefore able to learn to read before the age of six, and forbidding them the opportunity may result in loss of the child's enthusiasm. Some children are not mature enough or able until after the age of six, and to attempt to teach them at the age of six may be overfrustrating. With the aid of reading readiness tests and the wisdom of his experience, the teacher will eventually learn to estimate the maturity of reading readiness of the child.

A related principle for the teacher to keep in mind is that maturation and readiness may be subject to external influence. The teacher does not sit and twiddle his thumbs, waiting for the child to say, "Okay, I'm ready now." He recognizes that adequate diet, general health, ear- and eye-exercise games, and a building-in of the desire to learn to read can contribute greatly to maturation and readiness.

Turning from our discussion of the application of the principle of maturation to reading, we want to reiterate that the recognition and understanding of it may save much wear and tear for parents, teachers, and children. One shudders to think of all the indigestion that has been caused by weary fathers who have created scenes when a two-year-old with inadequately developed finger coordination has not used a fork properly. On the other hand, it is equally dismaying to behold the child of twelve with no table manners because his "modern parents" ignored the point of his growth at which he was ready to be taught table manners. The same can be said for every aspect of human learning. It seems wasteful to try to "socialize" a young child who has just reached the developmental stage of playing by himself or beside (not with) another child in nursery school. One can capitalize upon the child's maturation level, though, by beginning to "socialize" him as he becomes aware that in order to build a house out of large blocks he will need the help of another child.

Teachers of older students are sometimes unaware of the maturation principle. They presume that students know scientific and literary vocabularies equally well and hence have reading facility in any subject. Perhaps the greatest self-deception that these teachers practice is that, because their course is required for graduation, the student is *per se* eager (and emotionally ready) to learn the subject. Instead of building up an interest or emotional readiness to learn—which is part of maturation, as has been said—such teachers threaten failure. The consequence can be little permanent learning, as any graduate student knows when he tries to recollect information he "learned" in Psychology IA when his interest lay in Chemistry.

There are many other factors that a teacher through experience comes to understand in his assessment of the maturity level of his class. He makes the assessment with the help of testing instruments and the advice of specialists and colleagues, and by comparing individual children and groups of children in terms of his own experience. He will learn in time how to judge and what to do about the maturity level of those in his charge. He will recognize those children who are mature enough to go beyond the usual course of study. He will develop techniques of building up maturity and readiness to learn in children who are somewhat backward. How he does this is a matter of teaching methods. In educational psychology, it is the principle of maturation that the educational psychologist wishes to convey and not teaching methods.

In this chapter we have tried to make these points about the principle of maturation:

1. learning and teaching are more effective when the proper maturation and readiness level for any given task is reached;

2. maturation can be influenced positively by providing and utilizing a rich instructional environment;

3. maturation and readiness to learn are related to physical, intellectual, and emotional growth;

4. the evaluation of maturation levels becomes less complex and indeed almost automatic as the teacher himself learns to make estimates on the basis of past experiences;

5. when the teacher is able to do this and to apply the maturation principles, he will find that his teaching is smoother both for himself and for the children, since all individuals learn best when they are mature enough for the learning that is offered them.

INTELLIGENCE

Quite obviously the learning process is related to the matter of intelligence. Questions about intelligence—what it is, how we get it, and how it is measured—have long captivated philosophers, educators, and psychologists. Although intelligence is an observable phenomenon, it manifests itself in such various forms that an operational and useful definition is difficult to formulate.

Intelligence is far easier to use as an adjective of judgment than as a noun. If one likes someone, one likes to say that he is "intelligent." On the other hand, if one dislikes someone, one may say that he is not very intelligent or is stupid. The further difficulties in definition are illustrated by such common remarks as "She is intelligent when it comes to algebra, but she certainly doesn't know how to run a house."

The reader may wonder at this point whether one's intelligence is general or whether one can be specifically intelligent. Both research and everyday observations are not yet quite definite on this point, and one can build a case in support of either alternative. Thurstone [1] and others have postulated that there can be rather general qualities (called the global aspects) which

[1] L. L. Thurstone, "Theories of Intelligence," *Scientific Monthly*, Feb. 1946.

appear in the individual who has an aptitude for delimiting and solving any kind of problem and that there can be also limited or specific problem-solving abilities. Terman[2] on the other hand, maintains that the really intelligent individual handles all problems with greater facility than the less intelligent person, even if the problems lie outside his field of special interest. Terman's findings further suggest that the gifted person (one who scores very high on an intelligence test) deals more capably with life in all of its aspects.[3]

In everyday life, however, teachers continually observe inconsistencies in problem-solving ability within a single individual. The Phi Beta Kappa member may be puzzled by the operation of an automobile. The expert automobile mechanic may not understand causal relationships in history. The mathematics professor may see no logic at all in the laws of human behavior, and the psychiatrist may feel that he is reading Greek when confronted with the simplest book on calculus. To make matters more complex there is the bewildering question of whether or not intelligence manifests itself apart from social behavior. Is the otherwise brilliant physicist who is a boor and offensive at a party intelligent from the social-relations point of view?

The reason we are making such an issue of this point is that teachers must beware of categorizing a child as intelligent (capable) or unintelligent (incapable) simply on the basis of a score on an intelligence test or the teacher's personal bias. A "dumb" blonde may become an understanding and efficient mother and housewife. A male student who measures low on an intelligence test may turn out to be a fine plumber or a good friend.

[2] Lewis M. Terman and Maud A. Merrill, *Measuring Intelligence* (Houghton Mifflin, 1937). See also David Wechsler's *Measurement of Adult Intelligence* (Williams & Wilkins, 3d. ed. 1944), Chap. 1, for another discussion of this subject.

[3] Lewis M. Terman and Melita H. Oden, *The Gifted Child Grows Up* (Stanford, 1947).

The reader should be aware that there is also some uncertainty as to where intelligence comes from. Is it inherited (a natural result)? Is it predominantly a function of favorable or unfavorable environmental circumstances—that is, of "nurture"? Is it a product of interaction of nature and nurture and, if so, how and what weight is to be given to each of the two forces?

Almost every discussion of this question, which is sometimes called the "nature-nurture" controversy, will contain some mention of the Kallikaks and the Jukes.[4] It may be recalled that these two notorious families, whose forebears were by and large feeble-minded, produced generation after generation of feeble-minded progeny. Their family trees were used by the advocates of the heredity school as clear evidence that one's intelligence is distinctly determined by genes.

Around the 1930's this position began to be challenged. The question was raised whether possibly some of the Jukes were feeble-minded because they did not have a chance (environmentally) to be anything different. The growing environmental point of view was able to produce some plausible evidence that children with parents presumably of low intelligence reared in foster homes with favorable environment grew up to be more intelligent than the "naturalist" would have led us to expect.

As might be anticipated, advocates of this position became as ardent in their beliefs as were their opponents. There were some "environmentalists" who gave the impression that environment was not only a significant factor in determining intelligence but could have an apparently miraculous influence.

In our opinion, the divergence between these two camps is well exemplified by the exchange between Bernadine G. Schmidt

[4] Leona E. Tyler in her *The Psychology of Human Differences* (Appleton-Century-Crofts, 1947) reviews the major researches on intelligence as do Anne Anastasi and John P. Foley, Jr. in their *Differential Psychology* (Macmillan, 1949).

and Samuel A. Kirk at one of the national meetings of the American Psychological Association.[5] The environmentalist's position is well represented by Schmidt in her study of children of low intelligence who seem to achieve beyond expectations if given the right kind of schooling and home environment. Kirk's critique, on the other hand, provides a basis upon which the student can evaluate critically the environmentalist's position.

Others have been concerned with this problem. Out of the University of Iowa, among other places, have come many thought-provoking comparisons of the intelligence scores of identical twins reared in different environments. These studies indicate that environment does influence intelligence at least up to a point.[6]

It is our own belief that the hereditary nature of intelligence is not yet fully understood and that environment may operate negatively or positively in its development. Our view is well stated by Gardner Murphy,[7] who says, in essence, that the complexities of the interaction between heredity and environment defy unraveling with our present research tools and methods. There seems to be no clear-cut way of determining precisely how, for example, the environment of the womb operates on heredity factors, and we lack instruments with which to analyze the gross or subtle operation of postnatal environment. Although the nature-nurture question should not be abandoned, it is our belief that it cannot be answered definitely at the present time.

But we are not taking a laissez-faire position. We are cautioning the teacher not to give up trying to educate simply because the child's I.Q. appears low. It seems to us that it is a teacher's

[5] See articles by Samuel A. Kirk and Bernadine G. Schmidt in the *Psychological Bulletin*, July 1948.

[6] Beth L. Wellman, "Iowa Studies on Effects of Schooling," *The Yearbook* (National Social Studies Association, 1940).

[7] See Gardner Murphy, *Personality: A Biosocial Approach to Origins and Structure* (Harper, 1947).

job to see how far the horizons of seemingly low intelligence can be expanded. Although the teacher and the parent should realize the truth in the folk saying that you cannot make a silk purse out of a sow's ear, we believe that there are quite a number of things and different kinds of purses that one can make out of a sow's ear. There are several implications here: there are sows and sows, and, more important, it is surprising what one can do with an old, dead, and to all appearances useless, sow. A good teacher can do quite remarkable things, in other words, both academically and otherwise, with children that other teachers have given up.

We say, therefore, that it is incumbent upon any practitioner in human relations, whether teacher, parent, physician, psychologist, or whatever, to seek for and try to provide the environment most favorable for the growth of any human being in his charge.

There are many children and adults with handicaps of one type or another who escape the fate arbitrarily assigned to them by parents or teachers or doctors when placed in a more favorable environment. Similarly, there are enough cases of individuals originally thought to be mentally deficient, or slow, or of average intelligence who turn out to be highly intelligent to support us in this position.[8]

The teacher, hence, does not naively believe that all children in his class will do equally well. On the other hand, he does not condemn a slow child to eternal "kitchen police." He suspects there are intellectual limits, constitutionally set, but he does not know specifically what they are for any child, and he knows that environmental changes can make surprising differences.

[8] We recommend to the reader Seymour B. Sarason, *Psychological Problems in Mental Deficiency* (Harper, 1949), in which is reported unexpected progress in children of low mentality who were treated by an increased vitamin diet, a more functional school environment, or psychotherapy.

If the definition of intelligence has its difficulties, it would be expected that its measurement is not a simple task. However, there is an abundance of intelligence tests on the market which are sometimes used with a religiosity that is destructive to their real value and detrimental to the individual tested. This is particularly true when strong emphasis is placed upon a score obtained from the test. Although it may be security-breeding for some teachers to know these scores and write them down on cumulative records, it is also necessary to ask what the figures mean and whether they mean what they are supposed to mean.

This is by no means to say that intelligence tests do not have their uses both in psychology and education. In the next chapter we shall discuss their value. At the present time, we wish first to familiarize the reader with how the I.Q. is calculated and then to mention some of the problems present in devising the instruments on which the I.Q. is based.

In calculating the I.Q., there are three expressions that the reader will have to make use of. These are *intelligence quotient* (I.Q.), *mental age* (M.A.), and *chronological age* (C.A.) and they are often combined in this formula for computing the intelligence quotient:

$$I.Q. = \frac{M.A.}{C.A.} \times 100$$

The term *chronological age* is almost self-explanatory. It is the life span between the date of the individual's birth and the date of the administration of the test he is taking.[9] For instance, if the individual were 11 years old, his C.A., regardless of his intelligence, would be 11.

Although the C.A. is identical for all individuals of the same age, the M.A. (mental age) is the attained or actual score that the individual makes on an intelligence test, which is made up

[9] Wechsler, *op. cit.*

of problems of graduated difficulty.[10] For example, the tasks in the test are arranged so that an average six-year-old can complete more of them than the average five-year-old but not as many as the average seven-year-old. Each task is valued with a certain number of month credits, and the individual's M.A. score is the total month credits accumulated on the test. The M.A. thus shows the individual's present level of ability.

Understanding the concepts of the M.A. and the C.A. should make the formula for the I.Q. more meaningful. The I.Q. becomes simply a number. It is a number that conveniently states the ratio between some score that an individual gets on an intelligence test (his M.A.) and the expected score of the average individual of a given life age (his C.A.) multiplied by 100 to remove the decimal. The I.Q., then, is assumed to tell us how intelligent an individual is compared with someone of his own age.

Although the calculation of the I.Q. is simple and mechanical, the devising of an intelligence test—or any test, for that matter—is a very complex task. There are many problems involved, and it is important that these be considered not only in the construction but also in the use of such a test.

First, since any test examines only a portion, or a sampling, of a person's behavior, we can legitimately ask whether the tasks required of a subject on an intelligence test truly indicate whether or not he behaves intelligently outside of the test situation. In other words, does the ability to solve problems in a test situation necessarily indicate that one can or cannot solve problems elsewhere? Another, and in some ways more serious, obstacle to the measurement of intelligence is the tendency of many such tests to require verbal responses to questions, whether written or oral, rather than performance types of response. It is possible that some people are more facile than others in their use of

[10] Terman and Merrill, *op. cit.*

words, although they may not be more intelligent. Certainly people who are deficient in the skills of the English language may be handicapped on an intelligence test requiring verbal communication.

Closely connected with this obstacle is the difficulty of creating a test which does not consist of problems most understandable to only one section of the culture. Allison Davis and his colleagues, among others, believe that intelligence tests tend to be culture-influenced.[11] The tasks themselves, the language in which they are couched, as well as the population upon whom they are standardized, are predominantly of the middle class. A middle-class child from the professional family is more likely to know more words on the vocabulary section of an intelligence test than the child from a home in which such words are not commonly used. Vocabulary tests can, of course, distinguish the intelligence of two children from similar backgrounds, but dissimilarity of background may affect children's seeming ability to respond to the items.

Finally, the emotional and physical factors—those present at the time of the test as well as those more permanently present—are imponderables in test construction. Some individuals are positively stimulated by a test situation; others are blocked by their anxiety. More important, an individual ranking high on an intelligence test may not perform in real life as adequately as his score would indicate because he is emotionally upset. It is entirely possible for a child to have the I.Q. of a genius and be unable to read because he is emotionally disturbed.[12]

The latter point brings us to the conclusion of this chapter and requires us to summarize our position. We have emphasized

[11] See *Davis-Eells Test of General Intelligence or Problem-Solving Ability: Manual* (University of Chicago Press, 1953).
[12] Robert S. Stewart in "Personality Maladjustment and Reading Achievement," *American Journal of Orthopsychiatry*, April 1950, reports a research which makes this point.

thus far the difficulties of defining intelligence and its measurement because in some educational quarters it is defined dogmatically and the instruments used to measure it are accepted without question. *This is not to say that there is no such thing as intelligence or that strides have not been made toward its measurement.* Intelligence exists and manifests itself both in the ability to see what a problem is and to do something about it. Some individuals have this capacity to a greater extent and more generally than others, but some, for whatever reason, have it particularly in special areas. Environment and heredity and constitutional factors are intermingled in its determination in an unknown manner and to an unknown degree.

Tests of intelligence differentiate roughly individuals with respect to their ability to learn provided that the individuals are of comparable backgrounds, have interest in learning, and do not have emotional difficulties which stand in the way of their using this ability. Intelligence tests are most profitably used if they are considered as indicators of the ability to learn the kinds of things taught in school and not necessarily taught in life.

A sober understanding of intelligence and its measurement may be of inordinate value in selection of methods of instruction and proper placement. For this reason in the next chapter we shall discuss in more detail the whole problem of evaluation.

Chapter 18

THE EVALUATION OF
INTELLIGENCE AND
ACHIEVEMENT

In the preceding chapter we discussed some of the problems which surround the concept of intelligence and its measurement. In this chapter we shall describe some of the ways in which intelligence is most commonly measured. Since almost every discussion of testing in the schools brings up the subject of achievement evaluation, we shall also discuss some of the uses and limitations of achievement testing.

We are introducing these topics here for several reasons. We have found in our teaching that students invariably ask questions about the measurement of intelligence whenever intelligence *per se* is mentioned. Furthermore, the classroom teacher often administers certain kinds of intelligence and achievement tests. Even if he does not, he presumably uses the I.Q. and achievement-test data which are recorded in the office files. Some under-

standing, therefore, of the derivation of the I.Q. and achievement scores will be of value in increasing teaching effectiveness.

CLASSIFICATION OF INTELLIGENCE TESTS

Intelligence tests can be classified in several ways. The classi-
fication usually serves to indicate to whom the test can be given
and in what way and under what conditions the subject is to
respond. For example, there are tests that are administered only
to one person at a time (the so-called individual tests) and those
that can be administered to a number of people at the same time
(group tests). There are those that ask the subject to *do* something (performance tests) and those that ask him to answer
questions, either in writing or orally (verbal tests). There are
tests that combine performance and verbal items. ("Item" is the
name ordinarily given the task required or the questions asked
on an intelligence test.)

One can see that individuals who can express themselves easily
in words are better able to demonstrate their intelligence verbally
than they can by doing things, and vice versa. Therefore, the
teacher will question an I.Q. score obtained on a strictly verbal
test for a child who he knows has language difficulties (is bi-
lingual, has a speech defect, or is verbally uncommunicative for
whatever reason). Conversely, he would wonder about the true
meaning of an I.Q. obtained from a test containing only performance items and given to a physically handicapped child.

The verbal and performance categories of intelligence tests are
by no means mutually exclusive. Both group and individual tests
may include both performance and verbal items.

All intelligence tests have in common the objective of presenting the subject with problems to be solved. It is a supposition that
his ability to solve these problems will indicate the ability to
solve problems in life situations. Tradition, research, and expe-

rience have rather clearly defined the kinds of problem that are commonly found in intelligence tests. Arithmetic items (in which the capacity to reason is presumed more important than knowledge of arithmetic), vocabulary items (in which the ability to abstract meanings of words is measured), tests of memory (which require the subject to repeat verbally nonsense words or random numbers), and items which test the ability to see what apparently unlike things have in common are characteristic of verbal intelligence tests.

Performance tests attempt to measure intellectual abilities by presenting the subject with nonverbal tasks. He may be asked to put together a kind of jig-saw puzzle within a certain time limit, to tap blocks with his finger following the same sequence that has been demonstrated by the examiner, to locate the missing parts of a body which is presented in pictures to him, and to arrange a series of pictures without captions in a sequence that tells a logical story.

The success with which the subject handles such tasks is assumed to indicate something about his ability to see relationships, to memorize and put memory to use, and to estimate how to act in an unknown situation, drawing upon past experience.

Two other factors occasionally give name and character to intelligence tests: time and power. Some tests emphasize that the ability to solve a problem or a series of problems quickly is an indicator of intelligence. These are called "time tests." Other tests give the subject as much time as he wishes, and here the emphasis is placed upon the solution of the problems without time limit. These are called "power tests." Many tests have both power and time items. It is important that the teacher recognize that a "nervous" child may do poorly because of the anxiety produced by the pressure of time. On the other hand, a glib, assured child may not have the patience which is sometimes required in thinking through and solving a real-life problem. There

are intelligent children who work slowly and become discon-
certed by time pressures.

THE STANFORD-BINET

The Stanford-Binet Individual Intelligence Scale[1] may be
called the grandfather of American individual intelligence tests.
Certainly until relatively recently it was the one most commonly used in schools, and a description of it is therefore in
order. It consists of a series of items of ascending difficulty. The
beginning of the test includes six items which the standardization
(prepublication testing on large groups of subjects) indicates a
"normal" two-year-old can do. It concludes with a group of tasks
(designated as "Superior Adult III") which the standardization
indicates that only a very gifted individual can accomplish. The
items at all levels tend to be more frequently of the verbal rather
than of the performance type. They include, at the simplest level,
identifying, by name, toy objects (such as a cup, spoon, cat); at
a higher level, explaining why it is foolish to tie a necktie around
your shoes, stringing beads from memory according to certain
patterns which the subject has been shown briefly; and at a very
high level, exceedingly difficult items involving abstractions (such
as figuring out the rationale of rates of growth, repeating nine
digits after the examiner, and duplicating a design from memory
after it has been briefly shown).

Wechsler criticizes the Stanford-Binet on a number of grounds
—the importance assigned to verbal abilities, time limits on certain items, and the tiresomeness of the tasks to many adults.[2]

---

[1] Lewis M. Terman and Maud A. Merrill, *Measuring Intelligence* (Houghton
Mifflin, 1937).
[2] David Wechsler, *Measurement of Adult Intelligence* (Williams & Wilkins,
3d. ed. 1944).

THE WECHSLER SCALES

Wechsler has constructed an intelligence test for adults, called the Wechsler-Bellevue, which can be given to subjects with chronological ages of fourteen and over, and one for children which can be administered to subjects as young as five. The latter scale is called the Wechsler Individual Scale for Children, ordinarily abbreviated as WISC.

Both children's and adults' scales are based upon the same theories of intelligence. Each is divided equally into performance and verbal sections, and yields a "verbal I.Q.," a "performance I.Q.," and an "over-all I.Q." Unlike the Stanford-Binet, Wechsler's test does not measure the subject's mental age. The verbal sections of the Wechsler tests question the subject on arithmetic, general information, vocabulary, similarities between things (such as "door" and "gate") and between concepts (such as "love" and "hate"), and what might be called ethical or social behavior (such as, "What would you do if your best friend accidentally stepped hard on your toe?"). In the performance section, the subject is asked to fit blocks, which are multicolored and have different geometrical designs, into a pattern like that shown in a picture which is before him; put together a dis-assembled puzzle; arrange in proper order a picture story; trace with pencil his way out of a maze, and so on.

THE GRACE ARTHUR
AND THE GOODENOUGH SCALES

At least two other individual intelligence tests are used frequently enough to deserve mention. One of these is the Grace Arthur Scale, which consists entirely of performance items and hence is particularly useful not only with individuals who are not verbally inclined but also with deaf-mutes and non-English-speaking subjects. The other is the Goodenough Scale, also wholly a performance test. It is considered useful for children chronologically younger than age eight.[3] The child is asked to draw a picture of a man and is given credits according to the completeness and accuracy of his reproduction.

GROUP INTELLIGENCE TESTS

With the possible exception of the Goodenough, the tests that we have just discussed must be administered by specially trained examiners to one subject at a time. Generally speaking, at least one college course is needed to gain minimum proficiency in administering, scoring, and interpreting such tests.

Since there can be real value in making an objective estimate of intelligence, and since the individual tests can be administered only by specially trained people and are time-consuming, it is the group rather than the individual tests that are most commonly used in schools.

There are innumerable group tests available. In general their items resemble those on verbal individual intelligence tests. Arithmetic, vocabulary, and manipulation of word concepts are the intellectual areas from which the problems are drawn.

Unfortunately, the score from these tests cannot always be equated. Records of I.Q.'s on a single child who has been given different tests show a widespread divergency. Therefore, the group test selected by a school should depend upon what the test seems to measure best. Buros [4] has compiled critical evaluations

[3] The Stanford-Binet, the Wechsler, the Grace Arthur, and the Goodenough, as well as other intelligence tests, are discussed in Florence L. Goodenough, *Mental Testing: Its history, principles, and applications* (Rinehart, 1949), and Lee J. Cronbach, *Essentials of Psychological Testing* (Harper, 1949).
[4] Oscar K. Buros (ed.), *The Fourth Mental Measurements Yearbook* (Rutgers, 1953).

and descriptions of group intelligence tests (as well as all kinds of other tests) which have proved helpful to the nonspecialist selecting tests.

USE OF INTELLIGENCE TESTS

As we have said, intelligence tests can make a real contribution both to educational and to clinical studies of the individual. A school may administer group intelligence tests at stated intervals to all children in order to gain a tentative estimate of each child's educational potentialities. But teachers must bear in mind that the I.Q. can vary from test to test and from year to year. Honzik, Macfarland, and Allen [5] have reported that even on the Stanford-Binet the I.Q. can increase or decrease as much as twenty points over a period of time. They recommend that retesting be considered every two years.

Equally important for the teacher to bear in mind is that a high I.Q. offers no assurance that a child will perform at the level it indicates, even if it is a sound measure of his potential ability to learn. A child with a high I.Q. may not be amenable to learning if he is emotionally disturbed or uninterested in the subject. On the other hand, a child with a low I.Q. may surprise his teachers with what he can learn if he is strongly motivated and effectively taught.

ACHIEVEMENT TESTING

Intelligence tests theoretically measure one's *ability to learn;* achievement tests are presumed to measure *what one has been taught.* As teachers began to question the objectivity of their individually and personally devised tests of achievement, the

[5] "The Stability of Mental Test Performance between Two and Eighteen Years," *Journal of Experimental Education*, Dec. 1948.

need grew for subject-matter tests that were more objective and more widely standardized. To meet this need, the "standardized achievement tests" were developed. Although most teachers still make up informal examinations based on material which they have taught their classes, they also recognize that there can be value in administering tests constructed by specialists. Such value lies in (1) the absence of bias, which may come from feeling personally involved with a child, and (2) the significance that may appear in comparing the children one teaches with other children who are learning at the same level. Reading achievement tests, for example, indicate how well a child reads in comparison with other children of the same chronological age and grade in terms of a "reading age" and a "reading grade," which are calculated on the basis of the score the child makes on the test. Through experimentation, the author of the test has found that the "average" fourth-grader, for example, will make such and such a score, the fifth-grader a higher score, and the third-grader a lower score. Thus a teacher can compare children in his own class with these "average" children.

It can be seen that such tests, if used wisely, can have considerable value for the teacher. Without them, teachers may overestimate or underestimate a child's ability and "homemade" tests may measure only those skills in which the teacher is especially interested. The standardized test is impersonal, and it measures many skills; many standardized reading tests, for example, evaluate oral reading, silent reading, vocabulary knowledge, and the ability to comprehend many different types of material.

Achievement tests have been prepared for a variety of subject fields. There are tests not only for reading but also for arithmetic, spelling, various social studies, and even physical-education skills, to mention only a few areas. Since there are so many tests to select from, the teacher is again referred to Buros [6] for critical analyses of the various tests.

In discussing the uses and limitations of these nationally distributed tests, it might first be mentioned that one's impressions of what children know are not always identical with what they do know. In reading, the teacher is chiefly interested in the child's ability to understand what he reads, but he may think that the child understands better than he actually does simply because he pronounces words with facility—or less than he actually does simply because the child stumbles when he reads aloud. The standardized achievement tests may give the teacher a clue to the child's true achievement in reading comprehension, since they measure more than oral reading ability.

The tests also have value, if given near the beginning of the term, in telling the teacher the level of difficulty at which he should begin teaching either individuals or classes. There is no point in attempting to teach a class higher arithmetical processes if the standardized tests indicate deficiencies in knowledge in the fundamental processes. Furthermore, since most classes are not homogeneous in achievement, the achievement test administered at the beginning of the term may provide a convenient and objective basis for estimating the achievement level each child has reached. On this basis, the teacher may group the members of the class for more effective learning.

Tests administered at the end or near the end of the term also may offer some measure of how effective teaching has been.[7] If there has been no improvement, the teacher may legitimately

[6] Buros, *op. cit.*

[7] Reading and arithmetic achievement tests are fairly typical of all educational standardized achievement tests. Discussions of them will be found in David Russell, *Children Learn to Read* (Ginn, 1949) ; Constance McCullough *et al., Problems in the Improvement of Reading* (McGraw-Hill, 1946) ; and Leo J. Brueckner, *Making Arithmetic Meaningful* (Winston, 1953).

ask, "Have the usual methods not been the right ones for this child or this class, or must the cause be sought elsewhere?"

Our point of view is implicit in the preceding paragraph. We believe that testing has only one essential purpose: to improve teaching. Some teachers seem to teach in order to test. We believe one should test in order to teach better. The comparisons that are made possible through the administration of standardized achievement tests allow the teacher to diagnose his teaching effectiveness. The tests may, as we have said, indicate to him what the child is ready to be taught and hence where he should be placed in regard to instructional materials and grade grouping. They may indicate specific strengths and weaknesses (such as mastery of facts in history). They may point to reasons for the child's deficiencies: they may, for example, show that the child can multiply but not add, and that this is why he is having trouble in arithmetic.

SUMMARY

Teachers will probably always want to evaluate the ability of the child to learn (intelligence) and the achievement of the child in whatever he has been taught. They will make these assessments both by informal tests and judgments (tailor-made out of their experience with each class) and by the administration of standardized, objective tests prepared by specialists in testing. Both methods have value for the teacher but in this chapter we have been concerned primarily with the formal tests of intelligence and achievement since the construction of informal tests belongs more properly in methods courses.

Our main emphasis has been to familiarize the teacher and the parent with some of the types of intelligence and achievement tests used and thus to bring about a clearer understanding of what they mean. We hope that in this way such tests will become greater contributors to the teacher's understanding of the child and hence serve to assist him in increasing his effectiveness as a teacher.

We have indicated that intelligence tests are not all the same and that therefore the I.Q. yielded by one test will not always mean the same as that yielded by another. Furthermore, the I.Q. can vary not only from test to test but from time to time. Since there are these variations in tests and I.Q.'s, the teacher must use the intelligence test with discretion and as only one part of his total study of a child or a class. He must check the group tests against his own judgment. If the results seem at variance with the child's performance, he should request an individual intelligence test. Even here he should recognize that individual tests have limitations and that consultation with the testing specialist will help him determine the significance and implications of the I.Q. The modern psychologist makes an evaluation of a child's ability to learn by using many measures besides the traditional intelligence tests.

We hope that no teacher reading this book will ever label a child solely on the basis of an I.Q. We further hope that he will never report a numerical I.Q., unexplained, to a parent, since this procedure may fill the unsophisticated or emotionally biased parent with gloom or seem to give him permission to beat his little genius until he behaves like a genius.

Our position in this discussion of intelligence tests and I.Q.'s is that the I.Q., if used cautiously, can make a singular contribution to effective teaching. It is our belief that in order to obtain its real value the teacher must always bear in mind where a particular I.Q. comes from and understand it in the light of other kinds of test results and the child's real-life behavior.

Much of what we have been saying about intelligence testing is applicable to achievement testing. We would add only that if the teacher keeps in mind the diagnostic purposes of achievement tests, even if the title of the test does not include the word "diagnosis," both he and his administrator will find that they can contribute much to improving the instructional quality of the classroom.

By "diagnosis" we mean that interpretation of scores an achievement test may: (1) show the teacher where to begin teaching; (2) indicate where specific educational lacks lie in the child's background (*e.g.*, he doesn't know his multiplication tables); (3) provide a guide for homogeneous grouping in a heterogeneous class; and (4) aid the teacher in assessing the effectiveness of his own teaching, thereby raising questions as to the whys and wherefores of either effective or ineffective instruction.

As with intelligence tests, achievement tests should be interpreted in terms of other test materials, actual performance, and teacher judgments. A child, for example, who reads many books and can tell the class intelligently what he reads can read well even if he measures low on a reading achievement test. On the other hand, a child who measures high in a reading achievement test but who never picks up a book unless he is forced to can hardly be called a "good reader" in one sense of that phrase.

Like to the good medical clinician, the teacher considers the result of an achievement test as one X-ray. More X-rays and other kinds of observations are needed before a judgment as to *what* is more important can be made. Finding out *what* is only the first step toward finding out *why*. And finding out why is significant only if knowing the why gives us some ideas about how to proceed next. If achievement tests, or any test for that matter, contribute toward this purpose, they justify their existence.

PART FIVE

Discipline

❧

Chapter 19

A PREVIEW

THE GREAT BUGABOO of student-teachers, experienced teachers, administrators, and parents is the problem of discipline.[1] In our experience no question is more frequently asked by parents and teachers than "What about discipline?"

Since no one seems quite sure whether children need more discipline or less of it, sometimes they get a lot of it and sometimes they get none. There has been much debate about its definition in recent years. Some educators prefer not even to mention the name and refer to an orderly classroom as one in which there is "good classroom control."

It is understandable to us why the inexperienced teacher worries over whether or not he will be able to control his class. He probably remembers the agony that he—or, at any rate, his classmates—caused some teacher who did not know how to discipline children, and he is apprehensive about being on the

---

[1] See George Sheviakov and Fritz Redl, *Discipline for Today's Schools* (National Education Association, 1944), and Robert S. Stewart, "The Problem of Authority: Parents and Children," *California Journal of Elementary Education*, May 1953.

receiving end now. He is also aware that regardless of the theoretical position of his supervising teacher, if his "discipline is weak," he may get a poor letter of recommendation and have trouble finding a job. On the basis of his own common sense, he realizes that school administrators are not entirely without justification in requiring "discipline."

His intelligence tells him that the kind of learning that ordinarily goes on in the classroom is impossible if there is chaos. A certain degree of orderliness and organization is essential to any forward-moving groups. Without these, there may be not only confusion but also an atmosphere of anxiety. No one in the classroom knows where he is going, and everyone gets in everyone else's way. The consequence may be hostility, directed toward the teacher or toward other children.

Unfortunately, the "teacher-to-be" seems to learn best about discipline during the first year or so of teaching. There is much trial and error that goes on as one learns the amount, degree, and kind of discipline that are suited to various situations and various teaching personalities. Worrying about discipline ahead of time does not help, but, although how to discipline is learned best in teaching, it may be helpful for the new teacher to have some theoretical comprehension of this problem. In this Part, therefore, we shall treat: (1) the psychology of the teacher's feelings about being a disciplinarian; (2) discipline through democratic control; (3) the psychological significance of teacher authority in the classroom; and (4) some techniques of discipline.

We believe that the teacher's feelings about discipline are basic. Many teachers are uncertain about how to be an authority, and they unsuccessfully try several devices to conceal their uncertainty. Some of these devices involve trying too hard to be poised or "strict" or "a good Joe." Many a strenuously poised or "strict" teacher thinks that if children suspect he is afraid of them, they will make the most of it. Therefore, these teachers expend a great deal of energy in <u>convincing the</u> children and himself that he is afraid of nothing. He believes that children are the way dogs are supposed to be: if they suspect or know (we are speaking about dogs now) that you are afraid, they will bite you on first glance. There is unquestionably a half truth here. The other half of the truth, however, is that bravado never kept a dog from biting anybody or a class from acting up. It is our conviction that the teacher will at least reduce the difficulty of achieving classroom control if he does not display braggadocio. Superficial strength is easy to detect, and if the new teacher puts on an act of being hard-boiled, he may simply be getting himself into hot water. Many adults can testify that it was far more fun when they were children to bait superficially aggressive teachers than those who were less pretentious.

Real strength and self-confidence seem to come from having at least some clarity and some inner conviction as to what discipline should be, from having some competence in subject matter and classroom techniques, some understanding of what children are like, and, lastly, some understanding of the psychological hazards that are present when one is first placed in a position of authority.

The latter aspect of the problem has great significance. Much of the confusion about how much and what kind of discipline parents and teachers should exert may be related to it. Perhaps some who were reared in strict homes and schools react against their backgrounds by moving foggily in the very opposite direction. They then find themselves in an untenable position of no discipline. In self-defense, they swing unsuccessfully to extreme authoritarianism.

Some perhaps have difficulty in assuming leadership roles (whether that of new parent or new teacher) because they are not sure of the esteem in which they are held by the children in their charge. They are terribly afraid that if they are assertive and hold to what they think is right, they will lose the love of the children. Most people seem to want to be loved, and the more unsure they are that they are, the more likely they are to believe that they have to purchase love. Our observation has been that buying love by making unrealistic concessions is an ineffectual way of maintaining discipline.

The question may revolve around the issue of whether or not love and respect are antithetical. It would seem difficult to love someone for whom you did not have some kind of respect. A new teacher seems to us more likely to be loved if he does not attempt to seduce the class into loving him by disregarding his own standards and beliefs. A parent who gives in against his better judgment and thereby appears in the child's eyes as insipid will probably be defeating his conscious purpose of winning the child's love. Perhaps what is psychologically fundamental is that it is difficult to have respect and love for someone who does not have some self-respect.

This is not to be misconstrued as an argument for either authoritarian or laissez-faire methods of discipline. We have been discussing some of the psychological reasons why discipline presents so many difficulties to the teacher and the parent. Actually our own procedural bias lies in the direction of democratic control, and since the word "democracy" is one that has different meanings for different people, we now wish to orient the reader to our general view of the relationship between discipline and democratic control.

Democratic control borrows some permissiveness from the laissez-faire (no adult domination) philosophy and some directiveness from the authoritarian philosophy but actually is something different from either of these. It is control which is exercised by both children and teacher, with the children consciously being involved in setting up standards and procedures and objectives and with the teacher guiding and directing out of his own adult experience and wisdom.

Possibly our concept is enveloped in Szurek's concept of authoritativeness.[2] He distinguishes between *authoritarianism*, in which control is exercised through use of a title or tradition or force, and *authoritativeness*, in which the leader is respected and listened to because of the competence and ability he demonstrates. A child does not respect a parent or a teacher who is irascible and erratic, or one who is rigidly punitive. He wants an adult who knows his own mind and also is not afraid to listen seriously to what the child has to say. The democratic teacher is neither a mollycoddler nor a dictator but is an able personality who is strong enough to act when action is necessary and to follow when following is indicated.

Democratic control is as much a psychological as it is a social and political concept.[3] It is not just a matter of techniques or of identical procedures in all situations. It is essentially one of building up mutual respect (which sometimes takes a long time). The forms and procedures may vary from teacher to teacher (depending upon his personality) and will vary for the teacher as he gains more confidence in himself. No one is more undemocratic than an authoritarian teacher trying to be the opposite, and nothing makes more for eventually embittered and undemocratic teachers than forcing them into more permissiveness than they feel they can tolerate.

We are by no means saying that an undemocratic teacher should or need stay that way. We firmly believe that democratic control is the most satisfactory solution to the problem of

[2] See Edith L. Ginsburg (ed.), *Public Health Is People* (Harvard, 1950), pp. 206-225.
[3] See *Growing Up in an Anxious Age* (National Education Association, 1952), Chap. 5.

discipline, but the teacher must move toward adopting it at a pace dictated by his own psychological realities and by the situation.

The goal of democratic control appears worth the effort. It seems to make teaching in the long run easier by reducing the discipline problem. The laissez-faire teacher goes home at night with his self-esteem severely damaged and himself worn out from being battered all day. The "successful" authoritarian teacher goes home at night fatigued because of the energy he has had to expend in controlling the children each minute. The democratic teacher goes home at night glad to take his shoes off, too, because all teachers are tired at the end of the day. But possibly he is less tired, or tired in a different way, because it is easier to work *with* people rather than *against* them.

The social argument for democratic control is that we are presumably preparing children to live in a democratic society. If they become accustomed to doing the right thing *only* because they are afraid to do the wrong thing, we shall be predisposing them to life in a totalitarian society. If such control were carried to its logical conclusion, there would not be enough police to go around. Although we should be aware that the absence of controls of any kind makes for anxiety and an underdeveloped superego, we also suspect that controls *entirely from without* have serious limitations, as is witnessed by the kind of driving that is done by so many people when no traffic officer is in sight.

We have not mentioned techniques, but we do not want to decry them. Various punishments have their place in creating order. They lose their force, however, when, for example, a high-school student has accumulated more staying-after-school time (sometimes called detentions) to pay for wrong-doing than is left in the school term.

In this chapter we have tried to do two things: (1) anticipate for the new teacher or parent some of the psychological hazards that occur when the authority role is assumed; and (2) orient the reader to the principles of democratic control, which, we feel, helps resolve the problem of discipline. We fully recognize that the phrase "democratic control" has multiple meanings and that the implementation of it is not easy. Therefore, we intend to examine the problem more closely, beginning in the next chapter with a detailed analysis of the teacher's role as the adult authority in the classroom.

Chapter 20

THE TEACHER AS
THE ADULT AUTHORITY

~~~~~~

SCHOOL ADMINISTRATORS sometimes accuse psychologists and psychiatrists—and perhaps not without some justification—of thinking only of the individual child and of forgetting that a teacher deals with a group of children as well as with individuals. Advocates of increased participation by children in classroom management sometimes confuse the teacher about how much authority, if any, he should exercise. In this chapter we shall make two points: (1) children in groups do not always behave the same as they do individually; (2) hence it is one of the teacher's responsibilities to exercise guidance, leadership, and authority in order that both individuals develop and the "good of the whole" be not sacrificed.[1]

[1] There have been many studies of leadership and groups in recent years. We select the following: Roy R. Grinker and John P. Spiegel, *Men Under Stress: In and After Combat* (Doubleday, 1945), an investigation of men in groups in wartime; Fritz Redl and David Wineman, *Children Who Hate* (Free Press, 1951), about groups of delinquent children; Kenneth D. Benne and Bozidar Muntyan, *Human Relations in Curriculum Change* (Dryden, 1951);

Teachers are aware that they cannot neglect the whole for any single part. Intuitively, good teachers have long realized that there is more complexity in leading a group than this simple statement implies. A group is not a constant organism, and a class shifts in mood, zeal, cooperativeness, etc. There are many reasons for these shifts.

Individual personalities both influence the behavior of groups and are influenced by membership in a group. We all know from our common experience that our "best" friend in adolescence seemed to change his personality and indeed was not our best friend when a third person joined what had previously been a twosome. Some women may recall a girl companion who appeared to be different people, depending upon whether she was at a "hen party," playing bridge, or at a dance where conquest of males was the objective.

Being in a mass situation can effect the individual's behavior in not always predictable ways. Since group life has particular intricacies, a teacher needs to understand not only the forces within the group that may be activators for "good" or "bad" discipline but also the psychological influences upon these forces.

Many forces act upon and influence the nature of the classroom group. Some of these are more or less self-evident: the quality and nature of the official leadership (the teacher); the nature of the unofficial leadership (the child or children whom the group looks up to); the physical environment(whether it is limiting or overspacious, underequipped or overequipped); the tasks to be performed; and the purpose of the group. A group is also affected by personality problems of the children; by its

Dorwin Cartwright and Alvin Zander (eds.), *Group Dynamics* (Row, Peterson, 1953); Alvin W. Gouldner, *Studies in Leadership* (Harper, 1950). All of these report the major thinking, theories, and researches concerning group process (from such places as Bethel, Michigan; Massachusetts Institute of Technology) as well as review the work of Kurt Lewin.

size (the optimum size can be decided only in terms of the purpose of the group and the kind of leadership); by the spirit of the group (which can be a product of such diverse factors as the weather, the proximity of Christmas or an examination, and even extraclassroom events—for example, wars and prosperity); and finally by the kinds of control and authority that the group has been subjected to previously (a stern father or a former teacher who was either "permissive" or "strict").

The adult leadership, for us, is almost the most crucial of all these factors, because the effective teacher is in a position to weld together diversity, reduce the anxiety which sometimes comes from excitement, stimulate interests in tasks to be done, or smoothly loosen reins which have previously been held too tightly. We shall try to clarify this point by some examples. An effective teacher will act with greater assertiveness than ordinarily if he recognizes that in a fire drill on a rainy day the class my be somewhat high-strung. He may intervene when the class is intimidated by a bully. He may make the classroom environment attractive for learning. If everyone has been under a strain for too long, he may take the children to a park where they can have much latitude without getting in one another's way. These are the things that the teacher judges out of the wisdom of his experience.

Although educators have always been aware of the importance of teacher leadership, concepts of it have changed. None was necessarily wrong; each had some justification in the social environment of its period, but each displayed its limitations when rigidly and unthinkingly adhered to.

Around 1900 the principal task of the public school was that of making, all within a relatively few years, a comparatively illiterate population literate. The purpose of the school was to teach by rote memory the basic skills of reading, writing, arithmetic, and spelling. Except for occasional parties, the daily routine was repetitious. Moreover, a teacher was not infrequently teaching a group that ranged in age from five to sixteen. It is not surprising that the role of the teacher had to be that of a severe disciplinarian. It was believed that if the teacher were "easy," the children would get out of hand—as, indeed, they did.

Inevitably a reaction set in against such authoritarianism. Educators came to believe that education for citizenship in a democracy required a more democratic classroom leadership and that education for thinking, which is so necessary in a democracy, could not occur when children were taught to obey without understanding why they should obey.

"Permissiveness" became the vogue and, as might be expected, the inevitable extremists moved to such positions as that of advocating that the teacher relinquish all control to the children. A classic cartoon in the 1920's was of the child in a "progressive" school disconsolately asking his teacher, "Do we *have* to do what we want to do today?" Of course, such phrases as "child centered classroom," "permissiveness," and "democratic teaching" came into disrepute both within and without the profession. Today, the problem of the teacher's role is under debate. Educators and the public as a whole seem to distrust the "too tough" teacher and the "too easy" one but to be uncertain about the psychology and philosophy of teacher leadership that is most beneficial for children.

Fortunately, there is a thorough scientific study of the problem of leadership of children. Lippitt and White, inspired by Kurt Lewin, made a series of investigations of the effects of different kinds of leadership on what they called "social climate."[2] Lip-

[2] See Ronald Lippitt and Ralph K. White, "The 'Social Climate' of Children's Groups," in Roger C. Barker, *et al.*, *Child Behavior and Development* (McGraw-Hill, 1943).

pitt and White sponsored the organization of four different clubs, each having a membership of five ten-year-old boys. These clubs were extracurricular and met for the purpose of pursuing crafts. Each of the clubs was comparable; that is, by the use of sociometric devices, children were distributed among them so that each club had the same balance of liked and non-liked boys. They were comparable also in social behavior, no one group having a predominance of aggressive or withdrawn boys, as determined by teachers. No one group contained more physically energetic children than another group. The membership of the clubs, then, was similar in personality characteristics, social relationships, health, socioeconomic background, and intelligence.

Each of the clubs was led by one of three different kinds of leaders for a period of six weeks. At the end of this time the type of leadership was changed. The physical setting, the clubhouse, was the same for all groups. Carefully trained observers sat behind one-way screens and noted in detail the behavior of the group and its members during all club meetings, and conclusions were drawn on the basis of these data.

The three kinds of leadership to which the children were subjected were called by Lippitt and White authoritarian (or, synonymously, autocratic), laissez-faire, and democratic.

Characteristically, the autocratic leader behaved much as one might expect. He structured the situation, telling the group what activities it would engage in and assigning to individual members the jobs they had to do. He ruled with an iron hand and tended to be personal, praising those whom he appeared to like and criticizing in a somewhat negative manner those whom he appeared to dislike.

The laissez-faire leader tended to let the children and their activities alone. He "permitted" all except dangerous activity and in most circumstances withdrew from his leadership role and did not encourage or discourage leadership on the part of the children.

The democratic leader was a leader-participant member of the group. His group met and first discussed, with the leader's help in guiding the discussion, what activities they should pursue. The leader did not plan for the children, nor did he leave all plans for them; rather, he was involved and consciously involved them in the planning. He helped them set goals and ways of achieving these goals, and he offered help in the execution of these goals when the children were lacking in necessary techniques. Although he was not impersonal, he did not play favorites. He had enough constructive criticism and commendation to go around; that is, each child was recognized for his accomplishments so that it was not necessary either to beg for commendation or to vie for it.

Lippitt and White's conclusions may have significance for the classroom teacher. They found more of what they called spontaneous cohesion (easy unity) in groups led by democratic leadership than in the other groups, more "we-ness," more mutual helping in setting goals and moving toward them, and more friendly and less hostile behavior. They also found less evidence of discontent in such a group.

The findings on the relationships between autocratic and laissez-faire leadership are provocative. Children seem to prefer autocratic to laissez-faire leadership. Although there was more fighting and disruption under the laissez-faire leadership, groups under autocratic leadership seem to react in two different ways. In one club under autocratic leadership there were frequent expressions of quarrelsomeness and rebellion even when the leaders were present. In another such club when the leader was in the room there was much evidence of submissiveness but whenever the leader left the room pandemonium reigned.

These conclusions may not be surprising to teachers. We know both as teachers and as former students that a weak teacher who seems to have no strength himself and is of no help is disliked by students, held in contempt, and actually creates in them a considerable amount of anxiety. A teacher who exerts control and gives direction, even though it comes entirely from him, is more acceptable. The teacher who combines both teacher guidance and child involvement is preferred. We know also that an authoritarian teacher may be very successful in dominating his class as long as he is present but that this class may "go to pieces" if his discipline is relaxed or he is absent.

The type of leadership that unduly restricts either psychological or physical movement is ultimately met by either retaliation or resignation on the part of the group members. Psychological restriction can occur not only where there is too much leader dominance and too little initiative allowed to the children but also when children are unguided and get in one another's way.

Opportunity for sociability appears to contribute to group efficiency. In the democratic groups in the Lippitt and White study, children who moved toward a goal which they had helped to set were not only more friendly but more purposeful when they were allowed to talk with one another than when they were required to do tasks without interchange of ideas.

Mutual setting of goals by leader and child may also be significant. In the democratic groups, as has been said, the goals were not unstructured as they were in the laissez-faire, or superimposed as they were in the autocratic groups, but were set by the total group, with the help of the leader. Furthermore, because of the leader's sensitivity, these goals were constantly kept in mind, and the children were able to gain some perspective on their progress. They *saw* that they were making steps toward their objective.

As in any research dealing with human beings, there are limitations to this study, and criticisms can be leveled against it: the groups were small; they were extracurricular; the "real" personalities of the leaders are not described, and so on. Nevertheless, there are implications worth noting for the classroom teacher. A new concept of teacher leadership is introduced which is neither laissez-faire (too often previously used as a synonym for democratic) nor dictatorial.

Thelen and Withall differentiate a "teacher-centered" and a "learner-centered" group.[3] Their conception of the two groups we summarize almost verbatim in the two following contrasting columns. The teacher activities on the left describe a "learner-centered" class and the ones on the right, a "teacher-centered" class.

Asks questions and gives information about the problem in an objective manner.	Identifies self with the problem and expresses a defensive attitude.
Evaluates the learner's achievement in terms of described objective criteria.	Evaluates the learner's achievement in terms of undefined subjective criteria.
Helps the learner identify a wide choice of problem-solving behaviors.	Presents a limited or no choice of problem-solving behaviors to the learner.
Facilitates the learner's free choice among problem-solving behaviors in light of foreseeable (to the learner) consequence.	Interjects own needs and tensions into the situation.

[3] See Herbert Thelen and John Withall, "Three Frames of Reference, A Description of Climate," *Human Relations*, April 1949.

Helps the learner to focus attention on the problem.	Avoids participation with the learner in problem-solving activities.
Cooperates with the learner in developing the solution to the problem.	Gives the learner considerable reassurance and advice.
Helps the learner to clarify the problem for himself.	Shows little or no awareness of the learner's emotional and ideational conflicts rising out of the learning situation.
Keeps pace with the learner. Shows an awareness and an understanding of the learner's overt expression of tensions arising out of the learning situation.	Sets the pace for the learner. Resists expression of conflict without helping the learner to recognize and to accept the underlying tensions and basic factors giving rise to the conflict.
Helps the learner to recognize and to accept an objective formulation of the factors giving rise to conflict and tensions.	

In summary, we have presented these points of view in this chapter:

1. in a democratic classroom the responsibility for leadership rests with the teacher;

2. this responsibility carries with it the obligation to sense when to be a "strong leader" and when to step into the background;

3. this kind of democratic leadership has as its objective the teaching of group control, which increases with age and experience of child involvement.

The last objective is not achieved in a day and so in the next three chapters we shall examine some of the ways in which we think it may be brought about.

Chapter 21

THE DEMOCRATIC

CLASS GROUP

DEMOCRATIC CONTROLS and democratic attitudes, we repeat, are not built in a day.[1] If they are conceived as feelings of social responsibility, they cannot be brought about through fear of reprisal. They must grow, and their growth is complex. Some teachers attempt to be democratic and, if they do not meet with immediate success, revert to authoritarian methods. Although they understand full well that it may take years for a child to learn the multiplication tables, they are dismayed when a class, after a month or two of democratic leadership, does not function in an ideal manner.

It is not sufficient for us to say that democratic teaching is complex. In this chapter, our aim is to analyze its complexity. We shall examine some of its components: the psychological

---

[1] We refer the reader to Herbert A. Thelen, "Human Dynamics in the Classroom," *The Journal of Social Issues*, VI, No. 2 (1950). Some readers might find useful Rudolph M. Wittenberg, *So You Want to Help People* (Association Press, 1947).

nature of democratic control; the flexibility of teacher leadership in a democratic classroom; and, finally, our operational definition. We know that the reader will not derive a blueprint from our analysis. It may though give him some ideas to think about as he reads and these can be implemented when he begins to teach.

A common fallacy of teachers who wish to be democratic in their teaching is that they mistake the form for the content. A formal democracy is not always a democracy. Some classes are democratic (in the sense in which the term is used in this book) without the children's ever voting or having a club meeting. Others are not democratic although the children go through the motions of elaborate elections.

Democratic control is, as we have said, as much a psychological and mental-hygiene concept as it is a social concept. Its core is in the feelings that exist between the leader and the group and within the group. If this kind of control could be summarized in four words, those words would be "feelings of mutual respect." In a democratic classroom, the children *feel* that the teacher respects them as individuals and human beings because he really does. They *know* the teacher feels this way because they are brought into the planning and decision and the evaluations of both discipline and subject matter whenever it is possible to do so. This does not mean that the teacher cannot make a move without asking the children what they want to do or what they should do. It does mean that the children discuss those decisions concerning matters within their scope. This does not mean that democratic discussions must be formal. Classroom parliamentary procedure, although of some value in adult groups, can stand in the way of free interchange of ideas.

Feelings of mutual respect which characterize the democratic classroom include, of course, not only respect of the teacher for the children *but also of the children for the teacher*. However this respect is based on his ability and maturity, not on the fact that he is the teacher. We are saying, in effect, that the kind of respect we are referring to does not come from sergeant's stripes or the policeman's club.

More precisely, he is respected because he can help point out where the bugs and the snarls are in their classroom activity. He can also *help* organize in order that things may run more smoothly and more effectively. He is adept at bringing out ideas from the children, yet, withal, he is strong enough to take command if things get out of control.

This latter is a very interesting psychological point. Children, like adults, sometimes act hostilely and in a manner in which they do not want to act because their own feelings get out of hand. It may be relieving for them to have a parent or teacher who can help them regain control. There are also times when children are anxious and uneasy, as in case of a war or other catastrophe, and they want a teacher who is able effectively to step in at that time. The teacher who is democratic is cognizant when such times occur, and he acts affirmatively. He looks though for the opportunity to return to the children participation in making decisions.

Finally, the teacher is respected because, in the vernacular "he knows his stuff." He comprehends his subject matter, or most of it. A child who is motivated to learn appreciates an English teacher or a social-studies teacher or any kind of teacher who has command of the material he is attempting to teach.

Nevertheless, we add parenthetically, new teachers should not be under the illusion that in order to be respected by children they have to know everything and know it perfectly. This is an impossibility for any human being. To pretend to be such a person probably puts such a burden upon one that the educative purpose is defeated. Students in teacher-education institutions sometimes seem to feel that if they are to be "respected" as elementary-school teachers, they must sing better than Lily Pons, do arithmetic with more ease than Einstein, know more about the social sciences than a Harvard professor, write well enough to take all the blue ribbons at the state fair, and play games skillfully enough to be on every All-American team. This is not only too much of a strain for the human organism but as an unattainable ideal it probably would produce a lot of nonentities who have no specialties or skills—or pleasures.

As a matter of fact, although children want and respect a teacher who is competent in what he is supposed to teach, they can also gain something from learning that a teacher has some fallibility and some limitations and the teacher's feelings about these. This contention represents a mental-hygiene point of view which has implications for democratic control.

It is our observation that sometimes a teacher who can readily acknowledge his own imperfections gains in respect and hence in discipline. A by-product, from the mental-hygiene point of view, may be the learning children derive from working with a respected but admittedly fallible human being.

It is a truism that for this to happen the teacher must be more competent than incompetent. Our point is that a teacher's limitations can be turned to an educative advantage. A teacher who can admit that perhaps he can't throw a baseball as well as the biggest boy in the class is gaining the respect of the children because he is strong enough to say there is something he cannot do. Democratic control in our estimation is closely related to mental hygiene. It contributes to the development not only of controls from within but also and inseparably to increased self-esteem on the part of the children. Part of the self-esteem may grow from seeing a respected teacher who is imperfect, thereby creating in the child an awareness that he can be good without always having to be best. We are all conscious, especially those of us who are in the teaching profession, that psychological difficulty may be caused by a compelling need to be perfect and a feeling of misery and inadequacy if one is not.

The essence of the last several paragraphs has been that a democratic teacher has assurance and exercises it but need not be flawless and moreover may contribute to the emotional well-being of children by being this kind of human being.

We want to make one final statement about a quite different characteristic of a democratic classroom teacher. We believe that he will most effectively put the principles we have discussed into practice if he has an assimilated understanding of child development, for then he will know what ordinarily can be expected from first-graders or adolescents or whatever age group he is teaching. He will not, for example, expect too much group cohesion from kindergartners, who are not so "socially" developed as nine-year-olds. He will be aware of some of the inner turmoils of high-school juniors which may make for capriciousness. Knowing what children are like at different stages of development, he will not be naive or overdemanding in his expectations. If he combines this knowledge with knowledge of what makes for group morale, and other elements that are characteristic of groups, he will be better able to provide what we have termed democratic leadership.

He therefore (1) understands the need that children have for adult leadership; (2) understands individual psychology in the various developmental stages which influences the kind and degree of leadership he must take; and (3) recognizes that a group can be a powerful factor either negatively or positively.

In regard to the latter point, a democratic group has the feeling of working together, pride in its accomplishments and a sense of unity. It contributes to its own control and reduces the need for authoritarianism.

Lastly, we remind the teacher who wants to be democratic that democratic control is interrelated with curriculum problems, including principles of educational psychology. The best-intentioned "democratic" teacher may meet formidable obstacles if he forgets the principles of learning or tries to teach a curriculum which is utterly meaningless to the children.

In summary, a democratic group is characterized by:

1. feelings of respect from the teacher, for the teacher, for itself, and among members;

2. the understanding of the teacher of complexities of leadership and group interaction;

3. the provision of a classroom environment conducive to an interest in learning.

What forms a democratic classroom takes are less relevant than these characteristics. There can, indeed, be many forms and ways of organizing such a classroom, and some of these we shall treat in our next chapter.

Chapter 22

DEMOCRATIC FORMS

TECHNIQUES or forms in themselves are no insurance of success. This cannot be said too often, because so many teachers, psychologists, ministers, lawyers, and others engaged in professions dealing with people are taught techniques and then are disappointed because they do not work out for them as well as they did for their teachers.[1]

Again this is not surprising. A tool, such as a chisel, does not do the same job for two different people. Not only must training be taken into consideration but also special proficiency (which is beyond training), mood at the moment, the quality of the materials worked on, and even such factors as the weather.

[1] As we shall point out in this chapter, each teacher builds his own democratic forms. The following references, therefore, are suggestive of ideas rather than documentation: *Were We Guinea Pigs?* (Holt, 1938) by the Class of 1938, University High School, The Ohio State University, is a stimulating and specific account of how one high school tried to build a democratic organization; Joseph Smith, *Student Councils for Our Times* (Teachers College, Columbia University, 1951), is an account of the high-school student council; and the subject is also dealt with in Robert S. Stewart, "Discipline," *1952 Yearbook* of the California Elementary School Principals' Association.

A football player who should know tells us that even passing a football is more than a technique. At a given moment, you must know not only how to hold the ball and how to move your body but the right psychological and tactical moment to pass, to whom to pass it (if previous plans seem to be blocked), and the direction of the wind. It depends, too, on your own sense of security.

This is by way of saying that although in this chapter and in the next we shall suggest some techniques for building democratic controls, these are only suggestions which must be modified by the teacher. These modifications will vary according to the teacher's own feelings, his background, his class, and so on.

In general, we can suggest three kinds of democratic forms. First, there is the informal discussion revolving around specific and general problems whenever they arise in the classroom. Second, there is teacher-pupil planning of activities, which we shall treat in the next chapter. Lastly, there are types of formal class organization in which the problems that face the class are dealt with. These forms need not be mutually exclusive. A formal classroom organization does not exclude the possibility of informal discussions when crises occur, and it will probably include teacher-pupil planning of specific activities.

Here are some examples of the flexibility of democratic forms. A teacher wishing to create an atmosphere of informal democracy might begin the process on the first day of school or in the third week if he feels comfortable doing so. We realize that many teachers are not ready on "the first day." For us the chief requisite is that he begin or experiment with a technique or method when he feels reasonably sure enough of himself.

He might, whenever the time is right, introduce himself to the class. He might tell something about his own background, though being careful not to monopolize class time. He might prepare for the semester's work by stating that he hopes that he and the children will have some fun and that they all will also learn something and that there will be good days and bad days as happens in any life experience. If he has spoken with friendliness, authority, and sincerity, he might then ask the children what they think makes good teaching—not what kind of teacher they like, but what kind of teacher they feel really teaches them something. The chances are that he will be able to make a list on the chalkboard of qualities that really make for good teaching.

But since we define democracy as a two-way process, with mutual respect and rights, it is only logical that next he would turn the discussion into what is a good class, getting ideas from the children and also contributing some of his own. This would be his opportunity to define his own standards of conduct and behavior. These lists of "good" teaching and of "good" classes might well be charted and kept in front of the room as a guide for both teacher and children. A laissez-faire teacher or a naively permissive one, in contrast, would not establish his own concepts of behavior. The authoritarian teacher would lay down only his own concepts.

Many opportunities for informal discussion may arise out of actual occurrences involving standards of behavior. Almost every class will present discipline problems—*e.g.*, some will not know how to walk down the hall; some will not know how to listen, and so on. As these problems arise, discussion can ensue and the teacher can direct it so that the class formulates, with him, the behavioral goals that it hopes to achieve during the year they will be together.

Goals and rules are psychologically different. Goals are neither resolutions nor regulations but are only aims that have been set for one or that one has set for himself. They are not something that one expects to achieve immediately, but something that one is working toward. Thus they are always stated affirmatively and not negatively.

A fourth-grade group we know used to formulate goals each semester which were related to actual classroom behavior. They were not imposed upon the class by the teacher. If a goal concerned becoming more polite, for example, it was formulated by the class only after it had become evident that shoving, interruptions, and other manifestations of rudeness were standing in the way of class harmony. These goals read something like this: "We walk down the stairs," "We listen when others are speaking," to mention but two. The goals were not evolved in a day but throughout the first month or even later. The teacher recognized that having too many goals could be frustrating and he was careful to see that the goals were attainable. They were quite distinguished from any rules and regulations which he may have had to make as the adult. Placed on a chart in a prominent part of the room, they were always before the class. Lack of progress toward the goal led to further discussion about how better progress could be made. As the goals were achieved, they were crossed off one by one.

Informal discussion can deal with topics other than behavioral standards: subject matter, a test which everyone has failed, or a field trip (why, and what to do about it). The significant thing is that the teacher leads the discussion so that the children have and feel that they have a real and necessary part in the discussions. The teacher who truly listens to the children will find that they have ideas worth listening to.

Let us turn now from informal democratic controls to the formal type. It is easy to help a class to organize itself into some formal democratic form. In actuality the class creates a "club" structure with officers, rules of procedure, and defined purposes. However, such a formal organization can become a hollow thing. A class may organize and have officers who do nothing. It is not uncommon to go into a classroom and see a list of president and committee members who never do anything except have their names on a chart. A class may also be over-organized. If it has more officers than there are duties for them to perform the whole thing becomes a farce. Finally a zealous teacher may unwittingly convey to the children the idea that their club has more jurisdiction than is realistically possible.

When organizing his class into a democratic group, the experienced teacher helps the members to decide what sorts of problems they can in reality deal with. They usually cannot change the course of study; they cannot change the hours of going to and coming from school; they cannot make decisions involving other classes; and so on. But even in the first grade or the kindergarten there are a number of matters that they can often decide: how to schedule the subject matter during the day, whether to go on a field trip or not at which place to have a picnic, and many other things.

In organizing a class perhaps the first step is to define together what problems can be dealt with. Next the class may consider the frequency and form of its meetings the order of business, and the manner of conducting business. In these matters, there is a danger of overformalizing and it is more effective to draw up "parliamentary procedures" out of the children's experience and to word them in language they can understand. These can be placed on a chart that is brought out at every meeting of the class. This seems more meaningful than the introduction of such adult procedural methods as are found in Robert's *Rules of Order*.

As the next step a class may decide the officers it needs for its anticipated functions, the characteristics required for holding these offices, and how often elections should be held. A fourth grade, for example, may decide to have a chairman and an assistant chairman (who acts as substitute for the chairman and who also becomes the chairman after expiration of the chairman's term). The class may also have a secretary or treasurer if there is a need for such officers and may decide to have the chairman appoint certain other officers. We have found that too much class time spent in voting can be boring, anxiety-producing, and self-defeating. The question of length of term of office is often an important one. It is our view that a two-to three-week period is advisable since this gives the opportunity for spreading the leadership.

In any organization of a class along formal lines, the teacher should remember that he must be prepared, if humanly possible, to follow any decision which he gives the class authority to make. It is damaging to veto an action simply because the class and the teacher are not in accord. This is why it is so important for the children to deal with problems and matters which are within their grasp and maturity.

Under democratic control, however, children will almost inevitably make decisions which, although not dangerous, later appear to them as mistaken. And such decisions should not be vetoed even if the teacher foresees the mistake. The class can learn much, for example by enduring for a couple of weeks a chairman whom they elected because he was popular but who turned out to be inefficient. Teachers may forget, in their eagerness to teach, that perhaps one of the best ways to learn is through mistakes. Planning a party and making obvious (to the teacher) errors in planning is one way of learning better planning. As an example, in one class the teacher turned over to the class the responsibility for planning the Valentine party. The committee appointed did nothing about it, and when Valentine's Day came there was no box for the Valentines. The teacher neither berated the children nor, at the last minute, made a box for them but calmly used their disappointment as the basis for a discussion on individual and group responsibility. Some adults complain that children do not know how to look after themselves, but it seems to be the tendency of both parents and teachers to step in and prevent them from making even harmless mistakes. At the other extreme is the tendency of some adults, when children make mistakes, to take punitive, angry, "that will teach you a lesson" ways of correcting them.

Classroom forms of democracy vary, of course, according to grade level. In one kindergarten a group of sixty children learned to choose two "chiefs" every week. The "chiefs," the teacher sitting between them with her arms around them in the beginning, did such things as lead the flag salute and call on children for telling what they had seen on their way to school. Before the semester was over, the boy "chief" was leading the boys to the boys' toilet by himself and the girl "chief" was performing the same duty for the girls, while the teacher remained in the room.

A class organization can deal with many discipline problems, both individual and group. But the teacher should beware lest the class become a court which metes out punishment. We know of a group of exceptionally bright children who sentenced a malefactor to be hung up by his thumbs in a stockade which they were going to build in a corner of the room. The sweat poured down the teacher's brow as he thought of what would happen if the superintendent should walk into the room. From every point of view it appears better for the teacher to orient the class not around the question of punishment, but around the question of why misbehavior happens (either to the group or the individual) and of what can be done to improve the situation. Children, both the culprits and the class, can be just as ingenious about making such analyses and suggesting constructive action as they can about thinking up punishments. Class meetings which are devoted to tattling, retaliation, revenge, and punishment are not really democratic but are actually the exemplification of mob totalitarianism.

In this matter of class control of its discipline, the teacher must remember that he is the responsible adult. Some children are so disturbed that they are constantly getting into trouble, and the other children are bewildered and disturbed by this. Repeated class discussion about a child of this type may be harmful both to the class and to the child. The mature teacher will in such cases find it necessary to say to the class that this is a problem that he and "X" will work out together.

We have suggested in this chapter that democratic controls can be achieved by both formal and informal methods. In either case the exact approach will vary according to the maturity of the class and the experience and confidence of the teacher as well as other factors. We have given some definite suggestions as to methods, but we reiterate that they are suggestions and not blueprints. In the next chapter we shall refine still further the methods of creating democratic controls with the teacher as the authority by examining in detail the avenue of teacher-pupil planning.

Chapter 23

TEACHER-PUPIL PLANNING

EDUCATIONAL THINKING on teacher-pupil planning has gone through a number of phases of development. It has extended from the one extreme, in which on the first day of school the children plan the whole curriculum, to the other extreme, in which the teacher presents a plan and the children politely adopt it.[1]

There are, however, some basic principles in teacher-pupil planning. First, if children participate in planning what and how they are going to study, they will feel and have a vested interest in it and, hence, their motivation to learn will be higher. Secondly, children have many excellent ideas which can contribute to planning. Many heads, if used wisely, are better than one. Thirdly, learning to plan one's activities is essential to mature living. Many adults who, as children, had everything planned for them may in their maturity lack self-direction and self-re-

[1] Successful teacher-pupil planning grows out of trial and error and application of the principles presented in our preceding three chapters. We can recommend, however, for specific help *The Teacher's Role in Pupil-Teacher Planning* (Teachers College, Columbia University, 1947).

liance. Such adults have to have their days planned for them and are at a loss when given choices or the opportunity to make decisions about how and what they are going to do.

The reader will recognize that these three principles really recapitulate in a somewhat different form what we have said in a variety of ways before. Again and again we have emphasized our belief in the importance of intrinsic motivation, our conviction that children's ideas are worth listening to and that maturity is characterized by self-reliance and a feeling of responsibility for one's actions.

We believe, furthermore, that teacher-pupil planning can make a significant contribution to the creation of democratic controls and thus to more effective discipline. If the teacher and the children plan together, the content of the curriculum and the procedures of learning are not superimposed but are arrived at jointly. This "jointness" may make for an atmosphere of "we-ness" which is the foundation of democratic control. The feeling of having to do it for the teacher, which can make for indifference or rebelliousness (which require the teacher's being autocratic), may decrease. If the children really have a part—and feel that they do—in the planning, this involvement may create a classroom atmosphere conducive to learning even in subjects unrelated to the child's present interests. The school day which drags on if the schedule comes from the teacher may lighten if the children can juggle the schedule within legally prescribed limits. It becomes more theirs and less his. Not only may democratic controls be more effective but learning more efficient.

As we noted in the preceding chapter, students' ideas are more sensible than adults often think. The acceptance of their ideas can make for better teaching as well as greater classroom harmony. Lesson plans become more vital because they are related to interests expressed by the children as they participate in planning. Children often have ideas which may be of diagnostic help in solving their learning or behavior problems. Many experienced teachers have taught with greater ease and better results after they discussed with their classes plans for improving everything from spelling to discipline.

Teacher-pupil planning, particularly if practiced consistently in a school system, can have an effect beyond the classroom. It can be a way of learning how to make decisions and how to abide by (but without rigidity) decisions which one makes with others. Because his ideas are sought out and listened to, the child's confidence in his ability to think and act upon his thinking may grow and last into adulthood. More subtly, by participating in planning and by evaluating the outcomes of the plans, he may better estimate the consequences of "wise" and "unwise" choices. He may come to see the relationship between decision-making and acceptance of the results of those decisions. Thus, teacher-pupil planning can contribute not only to more successful classroom control and higher motivation for learning but also to a healthy emotional life, in which neither authority nor self-responsibility is fearsome.

Like democratic classroom organization, teacher-pupil planning can occur in many forms and degrees. We shall take much of the remainder of the chapter to examine some of them and some of the problems involved. We again remind the reader that we are not offering prescriptions and that his own experience will be the best teacher. As in all teaching, we repeat, the teacher's personality, his teaching maturity, the class size and age, the socioeconomic situation, and even the state of the world must somehow be taken into account.

Teacher-pupil planning can be on a large or a small scale, formal or informal. On a large scale it is possible for children, although they will make errors, to plan formally the daily program. Here the teacher needs to be aware of certain realities. Since the course of study is set by law, it necessarily provides the framework within which children plan—so many minutes must be devoted to arithmetic, so many to social studies, so many to other prescribed subjects. But although the law prescribes both *what* and *how often* subjects must be taught, generally it does not prescribe the order in which they must occur throughout the day. Thus these matters, left to the discretion of the teacher, are proper materials for teacher-pupil planning.

It is germane to mention here that although there are psychological advantages in teacher-pupil planning of the daily program, it is not necessary to plan each day anew. Some overzealous teachers start each day with the question "How are we going to arrange today?" Such a procedure may lead to boredom on the part of the children and to "discipline problems." In "real life," routines are set. Likewise, in classroom life a daily plan that is usually followed can be arrived at early in the semester. The plan is subject to change if change seems feasible to all. Parts of it may daily be subject to replanning, but each day need not be planned afresh.

It is again necessary to state our hypothesis that human beings can learn from trial and error, and hence the ideal daily plan will probably be achieved not on the first day of planning but only through experience. An example of this occurred in a class of nine-year-olds who were permitted by school-board regulations fifty minutes of art a week. At first they chose to divide this sum by five, leaving about ten minutes a day for art. In a few days, they became aware that ten minutes was barely enough time to get started, and they changed their daily plans first to include several periods of art a week and later to one, since that offered them a longer period of time for creativity.

A democratically controlled classroom may adopt, then, a

usual daily program out of experience, but each morning, during the class business meeting, children have the opportunity to suggest changes in that plan and to give valid reasons for these changes. Holidays, special programs, and special opportunities may be sufficient reason for changing the usual plan. There is no reason why on certain days certain subjects may not be omitted and made up on a second day. This kind of planning seems both adult-like and sensible. It partakes neither of teacher-dominated planning nor the kind of chaotic upheaval which can become fruitless and irritating both for the class and for the teacher.

Planning on a small scale can be done when it is restricted to individual subject matter. This is more easily done in the social sciences, where more freedom is ordinarily allowed by the course of study. In some schools a teacher has a choice of several areas of study in the social sciences and may present the children with these alternatives.

In schools in which no choice is allowed, planning does not revolve around what to study but rather the approach to the subject: the teacher helps the children plan how to go about the study of a prescribed area. The class plans the attack and pursues solutions to the problem raised. Thenceforth, planning in the social studies becomes very simple. Each day at the conclusion of the social-studies period it is natural for the class to check its progress in solving the problems, and out of this evaluation to plan for the next day's activities. Good planning cannot be separated from evaluation. New principles and changes in old plans are dependent upon the evaluation of past experiences.

In subjects other than social studies, planning is more circumscribed. Even in a subject such as spelling, however, children can discuss how best to conduct a spelling lesson, or how to improve the class average. Poor results on an arithmetic test can be cooperatively analyzed and plans made for more efficient learning. There are, of course, numerous extracurricular activities which can be planned for—excursions and assembly programs, for example.

As in all democratic procedures, the teacher is on the lookout for those areas in which the child has sufficient interest to want to be involved in the planning. In teacher-pupil planning without involvement the obstacles to achieving "we-ness" may be too great.

In the discussion of some techniques of teacher-pupil planning, we hope that the reader has not forgotten our primary emphasis: discipline is a prerequisite in order that learning in the classroom and living with other people at home and in later life can proceed. Discipline means control and organization in movement toward meaningful objectives. It can be imposed from without entirely, either by fear of the leader or by group punishment of deviations. We believe with Lippitt and White, however, that the discipline that is most productive for the children and least wearing for the teacher or the parent has the characteristics of socio-psychological democracy. This democratic control is a joint enterprise, with the adult at the helm because of his competences and experience. There is involvement which grows out of interest in the task to be accomplished as well as out of the permeation of friendly and mutually respectful feelings in the total group. Various techniques (such as teacher-pupil planning) and various forms (such as different kinds of class organization) contribute toward the attainment of this kind of control. Most important, however, is the atmosphere that is created. The atmosphere in the long run frequently if not always depends upon the ability of the teacher or parent to adapt the theory to the life experience in which he finds himself, an adaptation which can only be obtained through trial and error on the adult's part.

Finally, we caution both teacher and parent that they will

meet or have children who depart radically in behavior from that which is amenable to either democratic control or the best application of the principles of learning. These are the children with exceptional problems, and every teacher and some parents meet them on occasion. They disrupt not only the theory but also the teacher as well as themselves and the group in which they hold membership. Closing one's eyes to the existence of "problem children" is unrealistic. Therefore, we devote the next Part to a discussion of the "problem child."

PART SIX

The Problem Child

Chapter 24

THE PROBLEM CHILD AND
THE TEACHER

IN THIS CHAPTER we begin our discussion of what is called the "problem child." [1] We shall define the term and then deal with the teacher's role as he meets such a child face to face in the classroom. In subsequent chapters we shall describe the methods that professional workers other than teachers use in their treat-

[1] There are many works that amplify the point of view that we take in this chapter. For an over-all discussion we suggest Charlotte Buhler *et al.*, *Childhood Problems and The Teacher* (Holt, 1952). S. A. Szurek discusses both traditional nosology and dynamics in simple language in "Psychiatric Problems in Children," *California Medicine*, May and June 1950. Erich Lindemann and Lydia Dawes report their studies on mild pathology in children in "The Use of Psychoanalytic Constructs in Preventive Psychiatry," Ruth S. Eissler *et al.* (eds.), *The Psychoanalytic Study of the Child* (International Universities, 1952), Vol. VII. For a comprehensive treatment of research in mental deficiency we recommend Seymour B. Sarason, *Psychological Problems in Mental Deficiency* (Harper, 2d. ed. 1953). Edith Gann reports research on a special but not atypical problem in her *Reading Difficulty and Personality Organization* (Teachers College, Columbia University, 1945). James L. Hymes, Jr., *A Pound of Prevention* (New York Committee on Mental Hygiene of the State Charities Aid Association, 1947), describes in everyday language typical problem behavior.

ment of "problem children" who need a kind of help different from that which the classroom teacher can give them.

In defining the term "problem child," we must first ask, "Whose problem?" Sometimes the problem is more the teacher's than the child's. "Naughty" and irritating children occasionally are so because the teacher is irritable or is imposing the impossible on the child. To use an analogy, some teachers, not surprisingly, whisper or go to sleep at dull teachers' meetings. These teachers are not problems. True, the teachers might exercise more self-control, but essentially it is the situation and their fatigue that cause the "problem." The parallel to the classroom is that some children are obstreperous or shy because of the classroom situation and not because they are disturbed.

It is not this kind of "problem child" with which we are dealing in this chapter, however. We are here concerned with the child who is unfriendly, angry, overly shy—to mention only a few symptomatic behaviors—even though the teacher is understanding and the curriculum is reasonably enjoyable and acceptable to the other children. We are referring to the child who is a problem to himself as well as to others.

TEACHER STUDY OF PROBLEM CHILDREN

How does one identify such a "problem child"? We believe that often the teacher can differentiate "problem children" by informal though careful studies of children whose behavior puzzles him. Such studies may (1) distinguish the merely irritating child from the real "problem child"; (2) clarify the cause of the problem; (3) point the direction of the solution—whether by the teacher or by a specialist. An unexpected result of making such a study is sometimes the reduction of the problem. The taking of special interest in him may fulfill the child's need for recognition.

In the making of informal studies of children, there are many factors to be considered: the teacher's own attitude toward the child, the school's requirements, and the child's abilities.

In making an informal study, it may be helpful for the teacher to think of himself as a detective. He looks in the simplest way possible for clues which may explain whether or why the child is a "problem." Because he is not a specialist in making a case study and because he has many other things to do than spend an excessive amount of time studying a single individual, the teacher must begin his study at the easiest level. He can begin by thinking, as he drives to and from school, about such questions as these: Am I unfriendly or do I dislike this child not because of what he does but because of the way I feel about him—and if so why? Are my teaching methods right for him? Am I expecting too much or too little? Does he need my help in finding friends and truly belonging in the classroom? Am I retaliatory when he does something "wrong." In other words, the teacher tries to estimate how and why he reacts as he does toward the child.

The teacher then makes a plan of operation from his analysis. He attempts to modify his own behavior on the basis of this self-analysis. He tries to become less punitive, more consistent, more patient, and more firmly strict, the course of his behavior being determined by his "rethinking" about the "problem child." If modification in his behavior does not prove beneficial, he will search the school record file to see whether anything helpful is to be found there. He examines the I.Q. to discover whether there are any discrepancies among the scores, or between the scores and his judgment of the child's intelligence. He does the same thing with achievement-test scores. These test scores may show him that he has expected too much or too little of the child, or that the child's problem is connected with lack of opportunity to exercise special abilities, among other reasons. He particularly notes what other teachers have thought of the child as indicated by their comments or the marks that they gave him. He may find that things went well until a certain year. What happened in that year to the child? He may find that a certain kind of teacher got along better with the child than another. "Why?" he asks himself.

While he is using the central file, the teacher may look at the health records and subsequently talk with the school nurse. The health records may show that physical illness is interfering with psychological adjustment; that the child's teeth are hurting him; that he needs glasses; that he has begun a period of rapid growth which may be predisposing him toward temporary emotional instability.

With all this information in his mind, the teacher continues to think. Like the detective, he is formulating new hypotheses from a number of easily accessible sources.

We pause at this point to anticipate a question that is likely to be in the reader's mind: "But what do we do in the meantime in the classroom? We can't let the child throw spitballs and tip over the desks while we are making our study." No, the teacher is not and cannot be inactive during this period of investigation. Whenever the child's behavior becomes impossible in the class situation, the teacher must use expedient or opportunistic measures. He acts in a manner which works best for the welfare of the class, the child, and himself, whether it be making the child the class librarian or having him sit in the hall or lie down in the nurse's office. He hopes that he does not have to have the child expelled, but even this is sometimes the only way out for the moment.

Let us return now to our discussion of the teacher's study of the "problem child." If the problem persists after these preliminary steps, he begins to make more organized observations of the child's behavior. This does not mean that the teacher need trot around the classroom with a notebook in hand, jotting down everything the child does. But he can look and listen more closely than he did before. Looking takes on new meaning and purpose for him. He looks now to compare the child's behavior by himself with that in small groups and in large groups; with members of his own or the opposite sex; with adults as well as children; in the playground and in more formal work environments.

Whether the teacher writes his observations down or not is dependent upon the time he has. The important thing, as Prescott[2] makes clear, is that he see as accurately as possible what the child is really doing. In brief, he may find that he had developed preconceptions of a child's behavior which careful observations invalidated.

He may discover, for example, that an "undependable child" becomes dependable when given responsibility of a certain sort; that a boy who is a cut-up in the classroom is awkward and timid when he plays games at recess. These observations may give a whole new picture of the child and may lead him to the root of the problem. Discrepancies, unexpected insecurities, or façade aggressiveness may be revealing to the teacher in his search for the why of a child's behavior.

There are other steps a teacher may take in studying a problem child. He can talk over the child's behavior with his principal, supervisor, and other concerned teachers. In some cases parent conferences are in order, and in some systems the services of various specialists are available.

Such a study, which requires astuteness and interest but very little time or special training, may have these results: (1) the

[2] See *Helping Teachers Understand Children* (American Council on Education, 1945), a study done under the direction of Daniel A. Prescott.

child's problems—if they are not profound—may disappear simply because someone has taken an interest in him; (2) they may disappear because investigation of home life, objective records, and observed behavior suggest to the teacher more effective ways of dealing with the problem; (3) they may disappear because, by virtue of the study, the child becomes a three-dimensional individual, interesting and no longer simply obnoxious—the teacher's prejudices which made the problem behavior multifold dwindle and the child's need to retaliate dwindles also; (4) the teacher is in a better position to know what specialist to call upon for aid if aid is necessary; and (5) the teacher may better understand the social role which the child is playing and the influence the need to play this role has upon his classroom behavior.

SOCIAL ROLES

Through his study of the "problem child," the teacher may learn something about the child's relationships (and their psychological and social meaning) with both peers and adults. These ways of behaving interpersonally we call "social roles." They may be gratifying or appear gratifying to the child but in actuality drive his peers away from him, thereby negating his desire to be esteemed and to belong to the group.

Our premise is that if the teacher understands the reasons for the social roles of the problem child, he may help in effecting a modification of social behavior. This premise is based upon the belief that social roles develop, in part, from what a person thinks, rightly or wrongly, is expected of him by those who are emotionally important to him. If the teacher, by his interest in the child or by his authority, becomes such a person in the child's life, he may have the opportunity for introducing the child to social behavior that is not destructive to either the child's or the group's goals.[3]

A sensitive teacher who has in his classroom a child with a handicap will not expect the same performance from him that he does from the child's classmates in those areas affected by the disability. He will not pretend that the handicap does not exist. He will help the child achieve a role in which he does not need to exploit his handicap to gain the esteem of his classmates.

It should be borne in mind that the teacher can create not only "good" social roles but also "bad" ones. We are all familiar with the child who gets a reputation among the teaching staff of being a "bad boy." Each new teacher may be forewarned of him, and the first time he is even mildly mischievous the teacher is alert to head off any trouble because "Everyone knows that if you give him an inch he'll take a mile" and that "a stitch in time saves nine." Not only has this boy been cast in the role of the "bad boy" by his teachers but he is also so considered by his classmates, who alternately condemn him righteously or are delighted by his successful defiance. Since everyone has joined in the assumption that they have in their midst a "little psychopath" who is destined to set fires and run off with automobiles someday, it is not surprising that the boy comes to view himself as incorrigible.

There are many roles or social behaviors which problem children display in school: being overly tough; overly conforming; overly shy; overly indifferent to approval by peers or the teacher, etc. What does understanding of these roles mean for teachers? Understanding the "why" of the role may help the teacher understand why a child behaves in a way that otherwise seems pecul-

[3] The problem of the influence of roles on behavior is intriguing and complex. We suggest as references Theodore M. Newcomb, *Social Psychology* (Dryden, 1950), Chaps. 8 and 9; Clyde K. Kluckhohn and Henry A. Murray (eds.), *Personality in Nature, Society, and Culture* (Knopf, 1949), particularly Chap. 2; Margaret Mead, *Male and Female* (Morrow, 1949).

iar. He may recognize that the role satisfies for the child a desire to be accepted, and he may therefore help him find new ways of social acceptance. He may help a child who might derive social satisfactions from achievement in learning to give up his "lazy" habits. He may help the overconscientious student realize that he can be liked even though he does not get "all A's." He may help the continual fighter on the playground to learn that this is not always the way to become class leader.

Once he realizes that the way of life and the values the child brings to the classroom have reality and validity for the child, the teacher has made an important step forward in understanding problem behavior—for he knows that, like himself, the child will not truly accept the school's mores unless they prove socially meaningful and valuable to him.

Such a teacher will also know that if he expects the child to play a different role from the one he has played before, and if the teacher is actually influential with the child, conflict may be created between the teacher's expectations and those of the family or neighborhood. This conflict situation stems, then, from the child's realization that his mode of behavior (role) at school is not the same as that expected of him at home. The difficulty or impossibility of reconciling the difference may produce a great deal of anxiety in the child. A boy may be in psychological conflict when the school wants him to be polite and courteous and his gang expects him to be tough and aggressive. A girl may be involved in an internal conflict if the teacher expects her to be a little lady when her family admires and expects her to be a tomboy.

Although the teacher strives to avoid inducing or contributing to a conflict between home and school social roles, he must not lose sight of the educative function of the school. He contributes toward the creation of social roles that are congenial and flexible to meet all social situations. This cannot be achieved, however, by condemning a social class from which the child comes or its values and ideals. It can be done by showing the child the value of behaving in a socially useful and gratifying manner in various social situations and by giving him enough success in school so that he may become psychologically strong enough to harmonize apparently conflicting social roles.

Although they may not always believe it, teachers have considerable influence on a child's social behavior. It is a rare person who cannot recall at least one teacher who made a difference in the way he looked at himself and his relationships with others. We have all witnessed "miraculous" changes in the chronic "bad" boy or the "dumb" boy who ceases to be so bad or so dumb in the hands of a teacher who digs out what is promising in this child and nurtures it. Such a teacher's attitude and expectation, founded in genuine interest in the child, seems to modify the perception the child has of himself.

SUMMARY

In this chapter we have made the following points:

1. in every class there are children whose behavior is so far beyond the norm that they are not easily amenable to the methods of discipline which we have previously elaborated;

2. the teacher can effect a favorable modification in the behavior of many of these "problem children" after he makes a relatively simple study of them, a study which does not require special techniques or uneconomical use of his time;

3. one of the outcomes of such a study is a better understanding of the psychological reasons and motivations the child has for behaving in a particular socially unacceptable manner;

4. such understanding on the teacher's part may be the way in which the modification of behavior is accomplished within the classroom;

5. problem behavior is sometimes a result of conflict between social roles demanded in different kinds of environments; if such is the case, the teacher needs to search for ways to harmonize the roles rather than sharpening their conflict.

We maintain that some problem children cease to be problem children as a result of skillful teaching and understanding. We do not maintain that this is easy. Some problem children have built up defenses that are very trying even to the best-intentioned teacher. These defenses we shall discuss in the next chapter. Other problem children have psychological difficulties so profound that they respond only to a team approach by teachers, specialists, and parents. Such children are our concern in Chapter 26.

Chapter 25

THE PROBLEM CHILD AND
HIS DEFENSE MECHANISMS

It is helpful for the teacher in understanding problem children to know something, not only about the nature of social roles, but also about those psychological behaviors which are called "defense mechanisms."[1]

Defense mechanisms are used by all people, mostly unconsciously, to protect themselves against emotional wounds that may be inflicted from within or without. It has been our experience that children with problems are less offensive and more amenable to cooperation with their peers and their teacher if the teacher realizes that some of their "offensive" mannerisms, ways of speaking, and actions are really "cover-ups" or defenses.

[1] The reader who wishes a more extensive discussion of "defense mechanisms" is referred to Anna Freud, *The Ego and the Mechanisms of Defence* (International Universities, 1946); J. F. Brown, *Psychodynamics of Abnormal Behavior* (McGraw-Hill, 1940), especially Chap. 9; Fritz Redl and William Wattenberg, *Mental Hygiene in Teaching* (Harcourt, 1951), particularly Chap. 3; and Roy R. Grinker and F. P. Robbins, *Psychosomatic Case Book* (Blakiston, 1954).

Children cannot always say what they mean or mean what they say, for reasons that are at times devious and unclear even to themselves. These devious behaviors sometimes seem to be barriers in interpersonal and intergroup communication between the problem child and his school associates and family.

Defensive behavior is not restricted to problem children. Both home and classroom offer examples of what we mean. Father comes home and bawls out the children when he is really mad at his boss. Jerry tells his father he doesn't want to learn to swim even though he wants to very much, but is afraid to show himself inadequate. When the teacher is annoyed at the class after he unsuccessfully tries to explain equations, he may be hiding from himself his deficient knowledge about equations. The class misbehaves and baits the teacher, boasting how brave they are, when possibly they are hoping that somehow the teacher will become strong enough to exert the authority they are seeking.

It seems characteristic of human personality to build up a defense (or security) system as a protection against threatening external or internal forces. Even as the human organism takes precautions against bodily injury, so it takes precautions against emotional injury.

It was Freud who first evolved the theory that the ego, or sense of self, must protect itself from threats to security. He listed a series of psychological devices unconsciously employed for this purpose, and these he called "defense mechanisms." They are also often referred to as defense dynamisms and have been incorporated into the concept that every personality necessarily builds up its own security system.[2]

Later in this chapter we shall glance briefly at some of the defense mechanisms included in the Freudian doctrine. At this

[2] See Dorothy R. Blitsten, *The Social Theories of Harry Stack Sullivan* (William-Frederick, 1953), Chap. 2.

point, however, let us look at some examples from everyday life of external behavior which may conceal or disguise underlying feelings.

One of these would be the protesting, with or without conviction, that one is no good. This can be a very efficient way of protecting one's self from experiencing failure or providing an excuse for failure. After all, if the teacher or the mother or the father introduces himself at a bridge party as an unspeakably poor bridge player, what can his partner say if he trumps his ace? This technique might be called "I'll hit me before you can." It is not infrequently used (and we want to emphasize that it can be unconscious just as well as conscious) when children are learning to read and are not being successful. This "psychological logic" is not hard to grasp. Not only, as we have indicated, does the child provide himself and others an excuse in case of a failure, but also for some children it seems safer emotionally to be failures and never to make a step toward improving than to be confronted with the danger of maintaining their new-found success. Thus, a problem child with a high I.Q. can convince himself and the teacher that he is "no good" because basically he unconsciously feels he is not.

Closely related to the "I'm no good" mode of defense, but sometimes much more irritating to teachers, is the pretense of indifference. This pretense is expressed by the words "I don't care," which may actually conceal a great deal of caring. It, too, is often calculated to save one from the loss of esteem in the event of failure. In fact, people who protest both their lack of competence and their indifference may, though not always, secretly wish that others would urge them on if their failures will not be held against them. "I don't care" may be voiced by the teacher when he feels inadequate about applying a mental-hygiene point of view or trying a new instructional method which he would rather like to do if he only felt more sure of himself. A nine-year-old whose parents have academic expectations for him that he feels he cannot live up to may say he doesn't care about learning—and say it with a chip on his shoulder. It is probable that a shrug of the shoulders and a protest of lack of interest and concern more often than not hide the opposite desire.

The last and perhaps most deceptive of the three everyday defensive behaviors we are now discussing is the "I'm better than you are" routine. Aggressive people so intimidate more submissive individuals that it is difficult for the latter to realize that the boaster, the braggart, and the person who loudly proclaims how virtuous he is may in truth (though unconsciously) be trying to prove himself to himself. This is psychologically comparable to whistling in the dark as a way of getting one's self past a cemetery. Teachers dealing with problem children need to be aware of this mechanism, as it not infrequently covers a very deep-seated sense of inadequacy.

Let us now turn briefly to a more formal examination of what psychologists term defense mechanisms. We shall name several but by no means all of these mechanisms. We have selected those which we feel have the most relevance for the teacher. We shall omit here the mechanism of repression (the denial of the existence of a threatening force) because, although it is relevant, we discussed it in Chapter 2.

Rationalization is the mechanism which seems to lie behind the behaviors with which we introduced this chapter. By rationalization we mean unconsciously giving to one's self and to others false reasons for one's behavior. The high-school senior tells himself and his teachers quite sincerely that he cannot concentrate and that every time he sits down to study he has to turn on the radio. He plaintively wants to know how he can get over this "bad habit." He is rationalizing failure because it is easier for him to accept the "bad habit" than the possibility that intellectually he does not really have what it takes to pass the course. The studious girl insists that she has no time for the frivolities of social life when the truth is that she fears she will be a wall flower at the next dance.

We shall take rationalization as a point of departure for a discussion of what we consider some rather important generalizations about defense mechanisms: (1) a defense mechanism is an attempt to resolve a psychological conflict; (2) as such, it may be "good" or "bad"—or "good" in one situation and "bad" in another; (3) the yardstick with which one measures goodness and badness, effectiveness or ineffectiveness, depends upon the constructive nature of the mechanism. When one gets into the question of "constructive nature," one is on shifting psychological ground, because "constructive" means different things to different people. What is constructive in one place or situation, moreover, may not be in another.

Returning to rationalization with these generalizations in mind, a teacher might be in a conflict over whether to teach music to his sixth-grade class or to turn that subject over to someone else. Fearful of attempting to teach music and yet unable to decide whether or not to, he would unconsciously dream up all sorts of reasons, which appear to him as valid, for or against teaching music. He may find he has run short of time, that he cannot locate a piano, that the pitch pipe does not work, or any number of other things. If the rationalization gives him time to make up his mind or to take training so that he feels capable of teaching music, we would say that it serves a useful purpose for him. If he only continues in conflict without resolution, constantly searching for new rationalizations, we would say that the mechanism does not serve a useful purpose. In other words, rationalizations which give an opportunity for an emotional recess in a conflict situation have their place.

Projection is another commonly used mechanism, appearing in teachers and parents possibly even more often than in children. The teacher thinks the class is bad or mischievous when it is really he who is resentful. A certain high-school teacher had tried job after job and, at the age of thirty, was still being indulged by her parents. At every faculty meeting, she took up a considerable amount of time haranguing about the lack of discipline and the plodding nature of the younger generation. It has been our experience that teachers in in-service courses who complain most about their assignments are most bitter about the laziness of today's children. We remember well one father who scolded his son severely when the son was sullen about returning to school. We found out that the father was just as reluctant, but ashamed to admit it, about ending his own vacation. In projection then, one ascribes to others qualities and feelings that one has himself and does not want to admit. The teacher who is reluctant to teach music and whose conflict is in part a consequence of his own monotone and who ascribes his not teaching music to the poor quality of the children's voices may be said to be projecting.

Reaction formation, another defense mechanism, is exemplified by behavior which is opposite to the behavior which one unconsciously both desires and fears. Many men in our culture, unconsciously in conflict concerning their masculinity, may behave overassertively and even cruelly. They take great pains to hide both from themselves and others tenderness and gentleness, which for them are feminine qualities. If the teacher we have been talking about would unconsciously like to teach music but consciously feels that to do so would betray his idea of manliness, he might react vehemently by being contemptuous of music and all male music teachers.

Compulsiveness is, typically, engaging in an activity, one might say, in spite of one's self. In other words, one *must* smoke even though one has a sore throat; one *must* do the dishes at two o'clock in the morning after the party even though there are no flies around and the family's health will be perfectly safe if they are not done until ten o'clock the next morning. Children are compulsive about stepping or not stepping, as the case may be, on cracks to "break their mothers' backs." Teachers are compulsive about margins being one and one-quarter inches wide, with not even one-sixteenth of an inch of variation. Compulsive behavior again is overinsurance that one will not give in to what one fears. Our teacher might demonstrate compulsiveness by doing what he unconsciously did not want to do (teaching music) with excessive thoroughness. He would probably drive himself and the children to distraction by insisting on using each minute of the allotted music time each day of the semester, singing the scales instead of popular songs, and being overly precise in grading examinations.

It is easily observable in everyday life that there are many people who use the mechanism of *compensation*—who must excel in one area to make up for their inadequacies in another. Two examples of compensatory behavior are the overachieving student and the overachieving athlete. This is not to say that all Phi Beta Kappas and all All-Americans are necessarily finding psychological compensation in their successes. However, many teachers will recall certain children who, apparently driven by an inner sense of inadequacy, have to achieve superior grades in all subjects. These children can be detected because of the tension under which they work and the extreme disturbance they manifest when they receive a B in any subject instead of an A.

Our teacher, disliking his lack of ability in teaching music, might drive himself to become the outstanding spelling teacher in the system.

An individual exemplifies *regression* by his return to earlier and often infantile or immature ways of dealing with obstacles. A classic example of regression has been mentioned in an earlier chapter but bears repeating here. The older child presented with a younger sibling feels left out and may try to handle the situation by reverting to bed-wetting, thumb sucking, or other behaviors which at one time in his life secured for him the recognition of his parents. Some adults also may regress to immature patterns of behavior if the way to achievement of goals is blocked. Some teachers may have temper tantrums when frustrated. Some mothers are prone at times to use tears to get what they want from either their children or their husbands. Some fathers can become enraged when they do not get their way.

Our teacher might regressively react to his *having to teach* music by throwing his pitch pipe on the floor and jumping on it.

We wish to repeat what we have already said in our earlier discussion of repression: defense mechanisms *per se* are not always "bad"; they may be psychological safety devices for survival. There is probably no one who can survive the stresses of life, the necessity for somehow managing libidinal impulses as required by social living, and the complexities of interpersonal living without at some time or another needing to find and use protective devices.

Our objective of discussing the defense mechanisms at this point is that many problem children have erected such monumental defenses against the outside world that it becomes difficult for the teacher to see through them. Characteristically, problem children will overdo indifference, aggressiveness, compulsiveness, or any other type of "cover-up" behavior. The consequences are two: (1) the most understanding teacher is deceived by the façade which covers up basic insecurity; and (2) the question necessarily arises in the teacher's mind as to the psychological implications and value of the defense mechanisms which the problem child employs. Our own point of view is that defense mechanisms in problem children are there for a purpose. The teacher may indirectly reduce a child's need for overcompensation or any other exaggerated behavior by attempting in the classroom to supply assurance, support, and stable authority. The teacher should keep in mind, however, that it is the specialist who makes a direct and frontal assault upon a defense system which seems damaging or restrictive to the problem child.

In this chapter, we have made the following points:

1. both children and adults are sometimes offensively defensive;

2. problem children have more than their share of such defenses, and the defenses of such children can make the teacher recoil from an understanding attitude;

3. if the defenses of problem children do not diminish as a result of a more congenial classroom environment, their cause may be deep-seated and diagnosis and treatment may require more of the teacher than he can spare in view of the number of children he must teach and his primary assignment, which is teaching. In the latter cases he calls in specialists who help in the diagnosis and treatment of the problem child. Who these specialists are and how they work form the subject matter for the next chapter.

Chapter 26

THE PROBLEM CHILD AND
THE SPECIALIST

As we said in the preceding chapter, there are some problem children whom the teacher seems to be able to help little or not at all. In such cases he resorts to other professions for aid. Seeking this kind of aid presents several questions with which we shall deal in this chapter: (1) What kind of help is needed? (2) Where can it be found? (3) How should it be arranged? (4) What happens to the child during his work with other specialists? (5) How can the teacher and the specialist work together?

The teacher will probably decide on what kind of help is needed in consultation with his administrator. This is sound procedure because the principal may have another perspective on the problem, may have special access to resources, and is often the individual who legally has the right to recommend extraclassroom work with the child.

There are many specialists who may be called upon by the principal and the teacher: speech therapists, teachers who are qualified to work with the mentally retarded, remedial-reading or other kinds of tutors, school psychologists, psychometrists, physicians, nurses, and finally those who work with children in what might be called the psychiatric approach.

Some clue as to which of these specialists should be sought should have been found by the teacher in his study of the child. Does he lisp or have a cleft palate? Does he seem not to have the ability to grasp academic questions and does the teacher want the objective evidence that an individual intelligence test may give him? Does the teacher want guidance in estimating the role played by basic emotional disturbance? Does it seem as though the child would be able to read if he were not handicapped by a physical or educational defect? If any of these questions seem likely to have affirmative answers, the teacher recognizes that his time and qualifications are too limited to permit him to effect a remedy. He therefore calls for help from those people who are specially trained to remedy the problem.

In some school systems, these specialists are legally and readily available. In such systems the primary caution is for the teacher to ask for their help only after consultation with his administrative officer and after someone (principal, teacher, or specialist) has talked over the matter with the parents. If parents are unaware that their child is receiving extraclassroom aid, their understandable antagonism may prove more damaging to the child's progress than any amount of special aid. It is just plain courtesy to try to work with parents rather than against them, although we know that occasionally there are parents who do not want to be worked with. If the parents prove to be of the latter type, it is even more important that the decision about what to do be made with administrative support.

In those school systems in which specialists' help is unavailable, the problem of where to seek it must first be solved. If the child seems to need treatment by a physician, the parents may have one of their own choice or an appeal for advice can be made to the local office of the American Medical Association. Many schools have part-time school physicians and full-time registered nurses who can administer certain kinds of treatment. Reputable speech therapists, psychological workers, and even tutors are either known in the community or can be recommended by neighboring universities or colleges or by branches of the state mental-health societies or state mental-health departments which are sometimes connected with state departments of education. If the teacher, in cooperation with the school administration, asks such sources for recommendations, he will be more assured of receiving help from competent specialists.

Each specialist is trained to perform a particular function. The physician, with his instruments for studying bodily function, is in a position both to diagnose and to correct health conditions that may be causing or contributing to the problem. School nurses, with their long experience and training in observing children's growth rates, visual acuity, body build, and symptoms of physical illness, are in a position to estimate the role these factors may play in creating problems. They also are qualified to correct some physical defects and to make recommendations as to how and where others can be treated.

The speech therapist has been educated to measure the relationship between hearing limitations (by use of an audiometer, for example) and speech impediments. Speech therapists also are adept in training children to speak with more facility when their voice mechanisms are restricted either because of vocal defects, such as a deformed larynx, or poor control of the use of breath. The elimination of speech defects may often result in the elimination of certain problem behaviors.

Teachers specially trained in supplying reading techniques to children who lack them because of frequent migration or insufficient primary schooling, for example, can be of great help to the busy "regular" teacher. They know games that appeal to the slow reader and books that are remedial and interesting, and they can discover whether the child needs more or less training in phonics or in the detection of visual word clues or context clues. In some schools they work with slow readers outside the usual classroom environment; in other schools they act primarily as advisers and consultants to the teacher.

The teacher of the mentally retarded child is also a specialist. Ordinarily he has learned how to adapt the usual school curriculum to the slow learner and how to determine and set up the educational objectives which can be attained by children who are mentally retarded to various degrees and in various ways. Like any other special teacher, he may work either in conjunction with the regular teacher or in a classroom in which the retarded children constitute a group apart.

When an emotional problem seems dominant, very frequently the teacher will ask for the help of a psychometrist or a psychologist. These specialists have been trained in, among other things, the use of psychological diagnostic tests. They can administer and interpret individual tests of intelligence, vocational interests and aptitudes, and personality. They are familiar with such instruments, for example, as the Stanford-Binet, the Wechsler Bellevue, the Rorschach, and the Thematic Apperception Test. The latter two are sensitive instruments for evaluating personality in a special way, and their administration and interpretation lie within the sphere of these specialists.

This list of specialists is not exhaustive. The principal is a specialist as an organizer, as an individual with experience with different kinds of children, and as the legal liaison between the classroom and the outside world. The various supervisors (general, art, music, physical education, etc.) are specialists both in diagnosing deficiencies (which may be the cause of problem behavior) and in making suggestions as to how these deficiencies can be removed. The recreation or playground director, the probation officer, and the social worker are all specialists who can assist the teacher with problem children, since they observe and work with the child in an environment which is often very different from that of the classroom.

Even in the most impoverished community there are at hand specialists who can be of help to the teacher when he is faced with a problem child whose problems he does not understand. Sometimes all or many of the specialists we have mentioned will say to the teacher that the problem behavior requires the skills of individuals trained in psychological or psychiatric treatment. These specialists are, in some communities, relatively new and their methods may be obscure at times to the teacher who has not worked with them before. Therefore, we shall devote ourselves next to a discussion of such specialists.

It is not easy to describe what psychological and psychiatric specialists do when working with "problem children," since their functions differ according to the problem and to their own training. Some will make a special study of the child which is different from that which the teacher makes, using particular kinds of tests and interviews. From these data, they may make recommendations and suggestions to the teacher and to the parents.

Some will counsel directly with the child over a short or long period of time. Their methods of counseling will depend upon their training and their theoretical point of view. Counseling may consist of advice-giving, listening to the child talk, or helping him to understand consciously his unconscious motivations.[1] When psychiatrists "treat" the "problem child," they aim

[1] Perhaps the most succinct example of what happens in a child guidance clinic or a similar setting will be found in the films *Angry Boy* (International Film Board, 1951) and *The Quiet One* (Athena, 1948). More technical descriptions of the nature and theory of psychotherapy appear in Frederick H. Allen, *Psychotherapy with Children* (Norton, 1942); C. A. Whitaker and T. P. Malone, *The Roots of Psychotherapy* (Blakiston, 1953); Mark Kanzer,

at uncovering and understanding some of the basic causes. Their techniques may include conversation, use of games which have psychological implications, play with clay, or finger painting.

One of our purposes in describing the work of psychological and psychiatric professionals has been primarily to help build for cooperation between them and the teacher. We believe that, for the well-being of the child, the teacher should be familiar in general with the methods used by any specialist. This is one of the essentials of the "team" approach in working with problem children. Although the teacher does not need a detailed account of the work that goes on in the specialist's office, any more than the specialist needs to know everything that goes on in the classroom, both need to communicate and exchange information with each other.

Sometimes there are barriers in the way of communication between specialists and teachers, but these barriers may decrease if the teacher is aware of some of the reasons for their existence. Within himself, there may be an overexpectation as to results. Having passed the "problem" on (although this seems to be a very sensible thing to do), he may think he has failed and hence he may defensively wash his hands of the whole problem or look for defects in the specialist. The problem child often returns to the class appearing no better and sometimes even worse. If the teacher and the specialist anticipate this possibility together, there may be less resentment on the teacher's part.

The specialists themselves sometimes unwittingly contribute to the barriers. They have lately been placed or have boosted themselves on to pedestals. Their work may be either oversold or undersold. Some of them half suspect they are infallible and

---

"Psychiatric Case Studies with Teachers," *Mental Hygiene*, Jan. 1952; and "Basic Concepts in Child Psychiatry," Group for the Advancement of Psychiatry, Report No. 12 (Topeka, Kansas, April 1950).

feel defensive because they know they don't know all the answers.

A vicious circle is thus started. Teachers refer a baffling "problem" to the specialist, are annoyed at themselves for not having been able to solve it themselves, and may put the specialist on the spot. The specialist, in turn, may feel that as a "specialist" he must provide a quick and perfect solution, which in many cases is impossible.

We say that the teacher and the specialist both have a respect-worthy role in the problem child's rehabilitation. Both may gain from knowing what the other does. Both may gain from knowing that each has his own lacunae, limitations, and professional irritations, which may decrease by applying an interdisciplinary approach—*i.e.*, team work.

In this chapter and throughout this section on the problem child we have made these major points:

1. in many classes the teacher will have children who constitute problems, both to the teacher and to themselves as well as to the classroom group, which are not amenable to the ordinary correctional methods;

2. in such cases the teacher, upon finding that the usual devices of rewards, punishments, and encouragement are not effective, will informally study the child's behavior in order to devise special corrective methods that fit the special causes;

3. he recognizes that with some problem children this is a difficult task because the problem behavior is not infrequently covered up by defensive attitudes and mannerisms which try his patience, and that the defenses and the causes for these defenses must be understood before progress can be made;

4. finally, some children have problems of such depth or scope that the teacher needs the help of one or more specialists who can be of assistance to him and to the child in diagnosis, planning classroom treatment, acting as an adjunct to classroom

treatment, or carrying out the treatment in a specialized way.

The problem child, whether his symptomatic behavior is that of excessive social aggressiveness, withdrawal, poor academic achievement, tension, or academic overachievement, requires special consideration. He is not only a problem to himself and others but he is potentially a problem to himself as an adult and to other adults around him, and thus his problems are as much a concern of the educative process as are his failures to assimilate factual information which the school has been instructed by society to impart to him.

We anticipate here a question that teachers frequently raise: "Doesn't the family have any responsibility?" Not only does the family have responsibility but cooperation between family and school is often basic to resolution of the problems. Hence, in the next chapter we turn our attention to the relationship and the establishment of the relationship between parents and teachers.

PART SEVEN

The Adults Around the Child

Chapter 27

PARENTS AND TEACHERS

We BELIEVE that one of the essentials for the optimum growth and development of the child is good communication between the home and the school. This idea has been implicit throughout the book, but we want to amplify it now. In this chapter, therefore, the relationship between parents and teachers will be the central topic. We shall discuss and raise questions about (1) ways of establishing lines of communication (both formally and informally) ; [1] and (2) some of the barriers that seem to stand between parents and teachers.

Perhaps the problem of home-school communication in the present era will take on more meaning for the reader after a brief résumé of the historical evolution of the relationship between home and school. In an earlier period of American

---

[1] Katherine E. D'Evelyn, *Individual Parent-Teacher Conferences* (Teachers College, Columbia University, 1945), records parent-teacher conferences verbatim. Percival M. Symonds in his *The Dynamics of Parent-Child Relationships* (Teachers College, Columbia University, 1949) discusses some of the ways parents and children feel toward each other, and this may be helpful in helping parents and teachers understand each other. Another source is Norman Fenton, *The Counselor's Approach to the Home* (Stanford, 1943).

history, the school was an integral part, if not the center, of the community. The teacher lived in various homes throughout the year, and the schoolhouse was not infrequently a social center on Friday nights.

Living in such close contact with parents, the teacher had no problem of how to get in touch with them. In fact, his problem was probably how to get away from them. His personal life, his religion, his politics, as well as his views on nicotine were always under scrutiny, a condition which still obtains in some sections of the nation. Since teachers are people who like at times to have a separateness, it is not surprising that as schools became larger, around the turn of the century, many teachers were not unhappy over the fact that they saw less and less of parents.

Nevertheless, dedicated teachers and concerned parents recognized that schools cannot exist effectively without home cooperation. Thus there arose parent-teacher organizations, "public relations committees" in teacher organizations, and, in recent years, a tendency on the part of the school to restore face-to-face parent-teacher cooperation.

The feeling of need for this cooperation has led to experimentation with various methods of communication. Formal organizations of parents and teachers are not uncommon, and they are proving to be a common meeting ground and a source of genuine support for public education. One limitation, however, is the nonparticipation of many parents. Not uncommonly, in regular attendance is the same group of conscientious mothers. Some teachers complain that the mothers who "ought" to come to school are never there. By and large, many parents seem to come to school chiefly when there is an activity which directly involves their own children, and parents' clubs appear to be most successful and to have the widest appeal when their programs display children at work. Parents seem to prefer to watch their child, whether it be in the elocution programs of the 1900's or their modern equivalent.

Even at best, however, relatively few children can appear relatively few times on public programs and, moreover, such appearances necessarily often are spectacular rather than characteristic of what usually occurs in the schoolroom. Teachers, therefore, who want to meet parents and to be met by them do not wait for Open-School Week or for the monthly meetings of the parents' clubs. They augment clubs and programs by classroom activities in which the parents can be involved.

Ingenious and democratic teachers, for example, may work out with their classes general plans for academic progress for the year and then invite the parents on an afternoon to hear these plans presented by the children. Every child can legitimately have a part in such a classroom program, one group explaining what the class hopes to accomplish in arithmetic and how and why, another group doing the same thing for penmanship, and so on. At the end of the semester, parents are again invited to view a program similarly constructed around the question "What have we learned?" In between times, special classroom events, such as plays and parties, provide motivations for parents to come to school.

But no matter how successful are group parent-teacher activities, there seems often to be a need for individual conferences between parents and teachers. Parent-teacher conferences may have various objectives, and the objective determines how each will be conducted. There are conferences for the purpose of reporting on the child's progress, or to enable the teacher, through his better understanding of the home, later to diagnose a child's problem, or to facilitate work with the home in order to treat more effectively a learning or an emotional difficulty.

In the 1940's, dissatisfaction with the sterility of traditional grades led to a movement to replace report cards by parent-teacher conferences. In such a conference the teacher has the opportunity to elaborate on the child's achievement and progress. The conference also provides an opportunity for the teacher to estimate the child's background and its influence on his school adjustment.

In the 1950's, such methods of reporting were still in experimental stages; they seem to have failed where parents had been peremptorily ordered to school, or where teachers had considered them a burden because of lack of in-service education in how to conduct such conferences, or the absence of compensatory time off for the staff. They had also failed where schools had not realized that, whether because of tradition or other reasons, both parents and children cannot be divorced too suddenly from a written, concrete report of academic achievement.

The eventual form that reporting pupil progress to parents will take is a matter of speculation. Probably there will be many forms, depending upon the locality and the specific needs. There will probably be combinations of written reports and individual conferences, more of the former in the secondary school, and more of the latter in the primary grades. There will probably be considerable flexibility and a swing of the pendulum away from the point of view that individual conferences on a regular basis are a panacea and a "must." There are some children who get along quite well both at home and at school when the relationship between home and school is quite casual.

A need for conference may exist when (1) familiarity with the school will increase parental understanding of what goes on in school and facilitate learning; (2) familiarity with the home will facilitate the teacher's understanding of a child's behavior; and (3) conferring may lead to modification of undesirable behavior. When the teacher's objective falls under the latter two categories, the atmosphere of the conference will reflect the teacher's desire to learn about the child—*i.e.*, the teacher's intention is not to be punitive as was the teacher in the old days, when he "sent" for the parent. He is trying, and so states to the parent, to be a better teacher to the child and wants to get a picture of the child as a result of the conference. If plans are made by teacher and parent as to what to do, they are a result of combining the teacher's professional judgment with the parent's special interest. For such a conference to succeed, it should not be held without the child's being fully informed of its purpose and imminence. Otherwise the child may feel he is being "talked about," become self-conscious and distrustful, and react in a manner to aggravate the problem.

Since, as we have said, the teacher is not talking with the parent in order to be punitive, the conference should take place wherever the parent will feel easiest. It may be revealing to visit homes, but some parents feel distinctly uncomfortable if the teacher sees where they live. Conversely, some parents are honored if the teacher comes to them rather than vice versa. In any case, the conference should be pre-arranged, with the time and place suitable to both teacher and parent. Its aim is to learn "facts" about the child and to gain some understanding of parental attitudes. Its conclusion, if successful, would include tentative arrangements for a second conference, in which the teacher and parent would discuss further how they could work together to help the child with his reading, for example, help him to overcome either overaggressiveness or excessive shyness, or whatever the problem might be.

How much leadership the teacher will take in the conference cannot be predetermined. He will try to be naturally courteous, remembering that this is a human relationship in which genuine good manners are not out of place. He will be more aggressive or less aggressive depending upon the problem, the parent, and his own personality. He will never act routinely but will probably act flexibly and wisely if he understands the principles of leadership we have discussed in our chapters on teacher leadership in the classroom.

Let us now turn our attention to the psychological barriers that often seem to stand in the way of parent-teacher communication. Since teachers and parents are human beings, certain feelings of defensiveness may be present. For example, the teacher may be overbearing or abusive during a conference because he unconsciously feels uneasy talking with parents. It may be that when he comes face to face with a parent he is brought back to his own childhood. Not really convinced that he is an equal to the parent, he may be either overaggressive or overtimid.

A parent-teacher conference may have subtle psychological meanings for the parent. If there is a conference because the child has a "problem," the parent may feel guilty and responsible and act defensively, since the inference she may make is that she is somehow at fault. There is still a saying in some quarters which helps nothing: "There are no problem children, only problem parents." Such a conviction seems only to make the parents feel more vulnerable and hence more antagonistic. It is our opinion that although parents may help to create the child's problems, they generally do so not maliciously but out of a lack of understanding of their own problems.

At any rate, the child is not benefited generally by the teacher's condemnation of the parent. A parent-teacher conference should not be a court. Its purpose should be to find a way to help the child. If this purpose is kept in mind by the teacher, the parent may be less inclined to attack as a way of defense, and to castigate the schools because "the teachers are nowadays ill-prepared and overpaid." If the teacher understands the parent's vulnerability, he will not feel the need to counterattack and may thereby increase the possibility of achieving his prime objective, which is the child's welfare.

These are a few of the numerous and subtle psychological barriers that enter into communication between parents and teachers. We believe that they are best learned in pre-service and in-service teacher training by discussion of human relations and the sharing of life experiences. Parent-teacher relations can be improved if faculty meetings are devoted to the subject of parent-teacher conferences. Faculty discussion, exchange of experiences, and sociodrama, especially if a specialist in this technique can come in as a consultant, may increase the teachers' proficiency and self-confidence in this realm.

In conclusion, we are convinced that:

1. home and school must establish both formal and informal lines of communication if the child is to receive maximum educational benefits;

2. the skilled teacher will, not infrequently, conduct individual conferences with parents, appropriate to specific objectives;

3. skill in these conferences increases with the teacher's understanding of the parent's feelings and his own feelings and with experience and maturity;

4. this relationship is essentially and obviously one that contains all the pitfalls of human relationships. Teachers and parents are not a species apart, and in order to clarify this point we are concluding the book with a chapter entitled "Teachers and Parents Are Human Beings."

Chapter 28

TEACHERS AND PARENTS

ARE HUMAN BEINGS

IN THIS, our final, chapter, we want to make a point that has been both implicit and explicit throughout the whole book: children and teachers and parents (as other people), although different in many ways, belong to the same psychological species. Although teachers are professional people and parents have special obligations, having a teaching certificate or the status of a parent does not mean that one becomes more than human.

There are several fallacious ideas which are popularly imposed upon teachers and parents. One is that unless they love all children under their care all of the time, the children will feel rejected (horrors!) and end up on a psychoanalyst's couch. It appears that almost all human relations seem to be characterized by a composite of "liking" and "disliking" feelings. Even those married couples who are most congenial and secure find each other irritating at times. It is not surprising to us, therefore, that sometimes parents would like to send their children back to where they came from and teachers would gladly exchange their class for one from Timbuktu.[1]

As a matter of fact, adults have no monopoly on ambivalence (a composite of both positive and negative feelings). There are many times that children wish they belonged to the family down the street.

What is really important in these ambivalent feelings is that the positive feelings, as a whole, be more powerful than the negative feelings: that husbands and wives would rather be married to each other than not; that friends find more gratification than irritation in the friendship; and that teachers, even though the children may be almost more than they can bear on some days, get more pleasure out of teaching than out of selling insurance.

An opposite fallacious idea, in our opinion, is that teachers (and even parents, friends, and married couples) must keep an artificial distance between themselves and those who are in some way emotionally close to them. Some fiction tells us that the way to win or keep a mate or friend is to play hard to get and never to give. Teachers are sometimes instructed that if they are easy, comfortable, and warm with children, they will be taken advantage of. So, in some schools, we find barriers erected between teachers and children, lest the teacher be thought an easy mark. Teachers must always be addressed in the proper manner, must never crack jokes, must never chat or in any other way behave in a naturally familiar manner. Parents are told that if they spare the rod they will inevitably spoil the child.

It seems to us possible for two human beings to be honest, direct, and nondeceptive in their mutual affections without loss of respect. We believe that respect is not inevitably a result of

[1] See Margaret M. Heaton, *Feelings Are Facts* (San Francisco Public Schools, 1950).

keeping formal distance between one's self and another. Children can call their mothers and fathers by their first names in one family and the result is only a semblance of affection or they can in another family address their father as "Father" and convey considerable love. Pupils can call their teacher "Mr. Woodward" with contempt or with real respect, or they can call him "Woody" with admiration or ridicule. Distance, if it is artificially imposed, is not a requisite for healthy interpersonal relations, and love that is compulsory does not contribute to them.

The last fallacy we wish to mention is the assumption that teachers and parents who are worth their salt should never get angry at children. For some reason, expression of emotion seems suspect in our culture, and especially the emotion of anger can fill one with apprehension. It has been interesting to us to observe children encouraged to play a game hard, but reprimanded if, when they lose, they verbally display anger even momentarily. This is considered not being a "good sport." Somehow this does not make good sense to us. If the anger persists and is destructive to one's self and others, that is another matter. But anger, if it is not festering or destructive, strikes us as an expected consequence of disappointment or frustration.

Teachers and parents are sometimes led to believe that they should never be angry at their charges, yet children, being people, can be unreasonable or irritating. It would take a saint not to be justifiably angry when children repeat a behavior that is personally and socially unacceptable. In everyday life it seems that children who continually stir up trouble feel much better when the teacher or parent sets limits, even if in anger.[2] Not only does the justifiable anger give the child a feeling that

[2] This point is elaborated in Robert S. Stewart, "The Problem of Authority: Parents and Children," *California Journal of Elementary Education*, May 1953.

the parent or teacher has strength, but anger can be one way of telling an individual that you are interested in him. Real rejection is present when the teacher or the parent is indifferent to the child.

We want to distinguish between justifiable or rational anger, which we feel is almost inevitable in any close relationship, and irrational anger. By irrational anger we mean, in part, anger which is directed at the person or persons or acts which are not the real cause of the anger. This kind of anger can be very disturbing to children or to adults because they are recipients of hostility which is retaliatory and punitive and which they cannot understand since they have done nothing to "deserve" it. The feeling is of being disliked as a person, not for one's behavior. Irrational anger can be displaced upon a person because one is unable to place it where it belongs.

Sometimes, for example, teachers may pick on a child because his mother is an interfering, domineering, and influential parent whom they can't talk back to. Likewise, teachers or parents become angry at a child's manners and create an issue, not because the manners are that important to them but because the child's behavior has humiliated them when they (the teacher or parent) wanted to make an impression in front of their own parents, the supervisor, or visitors.

The problem becomes not one of pushing irrational anger underground but rather of dealing with it when it arises. It is our experience that if it is handled directly it becomes less destructive and tends less to feed on itself. There are several ways of dealing with it directly. One is by anticipation. A teacher or parent who can announce to children that he or she is in a bad mood, has a headache, or is irritated at somebody other than the children may actually so relieve himself of this tension that his angry feelings will disappear. At worst, the children will know why he is "crabby" and will not be wounded personally and be tempted to retaliate. They may even, if he has established any mutuality of respect, take care of him that day since he has explained to them that he has bad days just as they do, and they know he tolerates their bad days.

Teachers and parents who can deal in this manner with irrational anger may be teaching something that will vitally contribute toward the children's growth. Adults among themselves sometimes find it difficult to get over the barriers which such anger sets up. A principal, for example, may find it too embarrassing to explain why he was unfairly critical of a teacher on a certain day and the teacher naturally harbors some resentment toward him. Teachers working together preparing a program for the public get on one another's nerves and cannot talk about the reasons either before or afterwards, and sometimes weeks pass before they will speak civilly to one another. Examples are endless. People who get irrationally angry and cannot discuss it with the other person sometimes go so far as to break up an otherwise agreeable relationship altogether, or sometimes sulk indefinitely.

One of us had a teaching experience at one time which may serve to illustrate several of the points we have been making. It happened during the Christmas season, which, as all teachers know, is a time that often produces tension. In this school a program had been unchanged for at least twenty years. It was so special that it wasn't even called a program, but a "Ceremonial." Each year it had become better, and these teachers, having perfectionism as one of their neurotic symptoms, had to make it still better each year, although it had reached perfection at about the fifth year.

The "Ceremonial" included biblical speeches by twelve sixth-grade prophets. The senior author was assigned the task of teaching these sixth-graders to speak like prophets—no easy assignment, since no one knew how prophets spoke, and the diction had to be improvised. It was decided that prophets prophesied in a monotone but with expression.

After Thanksgiving the teacher in charge of the prophets (at this time the senior author of this book) would arrive at school to meet the prophets at eight o'clock in the morning, wrench the prophetic manner from them for an hour, and, exhausted, dash to his fourth-grade classroom at nine, taking just enough time to make an assignment to keep them quiet until ten o'clock, while he returned to the prophets in the auditorium. The assignment was always fifteen pages of arithmetic. For centuries it seems that teachers have naively believed that arithmetic can be an opiate for children. The reality seems to be the opposite. Left alone, children become bored and frustrated with adding and subtracting eternal columns.

As the teacher would come rushing up the stairs at two minutes of ten, he would catch sight of a scout or spy who had been posted outside the door to warn the class of his return. So when he entered the classroom all appeared quiet on the surface, but there was ample evidence that havoc had reigned. The children had forgotten to right an upturned desk in the back of the room; the eraser marks were still on the ceiling; a little girl's pigtails would be dripping with ink.

Already worn to a frazzle by the prophets, the teacher would rant and rave, alternately appealing to loyalty and "school spirit" and hinting broadly that such behavior would lead to all kinds of trouble. He invariably ended the tirade (which subdued everyone temporarily) by assigning thirty more pages of arithmetic for the ten-to-eleven-o'clock period (which he had to spend with the prophets) and promising that *anyone* who didn't finish *all of it* would stay after school until he had. Of course, at the end of the day no one had come anywhere near finishing his arithmetic, but the teacher was so worn out that he wouldn't have stayed after school for twice his salary. He would rationalize his "backing down" with "after all, one wouldn't want the little ones to cross the street and get run over at five o'clock when the traffic monitors had gone off duty and it was dark and rainy." Fortunately for this rationalization it rained almost every day during December.

Day after day went on in this fashion. The children became more irascible. The teacher developed chronic insomnia and became increasingly erratic during the daytime. Unable to tolerate the frustration any longer, he decided one day to stop displaying his anger and to try to get at the root of the problem with the class.

The teacher started out the next morning, saying something like this with the utmost sincerity to the class, "What's the matter with us? We used to have our bad days but as a whole we got along pretty well. I get crabbier and crabbier, and you get ornerier and ornerier. Let's talk about it."

The discussion brought about a joint understanding of both the justifiable and the irrational aspects of mutual antagonism. Since the teacher was strong enough to admit to his fallibility, the children seemed to become able to relinquish their hostility, which was present partly because they too had been somewhat in the wrong. With anger placed where it belonged (on the frustrations of the reality situation) it tended to disappear and the teacher and the class were able to figure out how to make the best of an irritating reality situation. (For one thing, the voluminous and pointless arithmetic assignments were discarded and more self-directing, constructive activities were substituted.) It would be untrue to say that unallayed congeniality prevailed from then on. There were still days when a desk got upset and the teacher threatened. But because all were aware of the real source of irritation, continual conflict was avoided.

For the "best adjusted" teacher or the "best adjusted" parent there are inevitable tensions which are inherent in the job and which cannot be relieved directly but which must be drained off. It is a truism for us that teachers are better teachers when they find ways of draining off these tensions before they affect their out-of-school lives.

Teachers particularly need outlets for their normal aggression. Irrational anger in the classroom, for example, may be avoided by laying in a supply of murder or adventure or science-fiction stories through which the teacher in fantasy can range far and wide. Burning autumn leaves, gardening, or knitting can be harmless tension-relievers.

Competitive recreational activities may reduce classroom tension. Some teachers play bridge with a vengeance; one we knew took up knitting, not only trying to make the *best* sweaters but also deriving a great deal of pleasure from jabbing the needles without restraint; and some bowl as if they were trying to shatter the pins.

In conclusion we want to leave both parent and teacher these concepts:

1. the relationship that exists between children and adults must be viewed as an interpersonal one;

2. parents and teachers as human beings will, in our opinion, become justifiably angry at their charges, who are other human beings;

3. they will sometimes even be unjustifiably angry but can retrieve the situation through honest and frank discussion;

4. tensions can be relieved in part by being able to be natural and self-respecting with children and in part by finding enjoyable ways of draining off tensions through associations apart from children.

Basic to all we have said in this book is the axiom that the most effective teaching is done by the teacher who finds real satisfaction in the work he has chosen.

RECOMMENDED READING

The following list is not intended as a comprehensive bibliography. In essence, it is a recommended reading list which we have attempted to gear to individual interests.

THE DEVELOPMENT OF PERSONALITY

Davis, Allison W. and Havighurst, Robert J., *Father of the Man* (Houghton Mifflin, 1947). Davis and Havighurst report in an exceptionally interesting manner the results of their investigations in Chicago on the influence of social class upon child rearing. Teachers who work with children from homes that are different from their own will find in this book explanations for behavior that might otherwise be difficult to understand.

English, Oliver and Pearson, G.H.J., *Emotional Problems of Living* (Norton, 1945). The impact of Freudian psychology upon the understanding of human personality can hardly be overestimated. English and Pearson discuss the emergence of personality from infancy through adolescence from this point of view. Every teacher should be familiar with the ideas presented in this very readable book.

Freud, Sigmund, *An Outline of Psychoanalysis* (Norton, 1949). Since Freud has been so vital in contemporary thinking about people, it is important for the teacher to know what the man himself wrote. This small book summarizes his theory as he saw it shortly before his death.

Geddes, Donald P. and Curie, Enid (eds.), *About the Kinsey Report* (New American Library, 1948). The implications of the Kinsey Report on sexual behavior of the American male are important for teachers. This Signet Book is possibly the best digest and interpretation of the report for those who are unable to read the original volume.

Gesell, Arnold and Ilg, Frances, *Infant and Child in the Culture of Today* (Harper, 1943), and *The Child from Five to Ten* (Harper, 1946). Gesell has spent many years in careful study of children's observable behavior and has arrived at several interesting and important theories about the way they grow. In these books the theories are discussed and, in addition, Gesell describes the "typical" behavior of various age levels. There is real value for the teacher in comparing the behavior of children in her class with the behavior reported by Gesell. However, perfectly normal children may differ from those Gesell describes. The so-called "norms" of behavior should not be taken too literally.

Integration and Conflict in Family Behavior, Group for the Advancement of Psychiatry Report No. 27 (Topeka, Kansas, Aug. 1954). This is a provocative and stimulating formulation of some of the psychological and social factors that go into the making of personality.

Jersild, Arthur T., *Child Psychology* (Prentice-Hall, 1947). For many years this has been a classic on child psychology. Jersild reports in detail what certain kinds of research have found about child development in many areas, such as physical growth, social and emotional development, etc. His chapters on maturation and readiness are especially helpful to teachers.

How Children Develop (Ohio State, 1949). This very compact book describes the health, security, achievement, interests, and appreciations of children—in infancy; early, middle, and later childhood; adolescence. An excellent book for teachers.

Riesman, David, *The Lonely Crowd* (Yale, 1950). As we have pointed out in Chap. 1, the cultural milieu cannot be ignored in understanding personality. In this book the author very readably describes what he considers the contradiction of the mass and individual nature of the American scene.

Spock, Benjamin, *Pocket Book of Baby and Child Care* (Pocket Books, 1946). This is a book which every teacher should own and have on his desk. It is a useful summary of present thinking on psychological aspects of child development as well as on physical disease, and it is one of the few books which teachers can feel free and happy to recommend to parents who are concerned with such problems as sex education, enuresis, handicaps (such as mental deficiency), lying, stealing, and a host of other problems.

Statistics Pertinent to Psychiatry in the United States, Group for the Advancement of Psychiatry Report No. 7 (Topeka, Kansas, March 1949). This report presents startling and revealing factual information on the incidence of emotional disturbance in the United States. Although chronologically the report is dated, the implications have not changed with the years.

THE CHILD AND THE GROUP

Allport, Gordon W., *ABC's of Scapegoating* (Central Y.M.C.A. College, 1948). A pamphlet discussing causes and methods of dealing with race prejudice. Simply and clearly written.

Frenkel-Brunswik, Else, "The Anti-democratic Personality," in Newcomb, T.M., and Hartley, E. H., *Readings in Social Psychology* (Holt, 1947). This chapter in Newcomb's book describes some of the findings of the University of California investigation into the genesis and kind of personality that is prejudiced and antidemocratic.

Helping Teachers Understand Children (American Council on Education, 1945). Chaps. 9 and 10 are devoted to the ways in which a teacher may observe and study a group, as well as to the importance of understanding how a group influences the individual. A simple description of how to make and interpret a sociogram is included.

Konopka, Gisela, *Therapeutic Group Work with Children* (Minnesota, 1949). Although written primarily for social workers, this is a useful book for teachers. The author describes in almost diary form how she worked with a group of delinquent children in order to restore some of their lost self-esteem.

Lippitt, Ronald and White, Ralph K., "The 'Social Climate' of Children's Groups," in Barker, Roger C. et al., Child Behavior and Development (McGraw-Hill, 1943). Lippitt and White describe in detail (in this book which also has other articles of value to teachers) their well-known study of how democratic, laissez-faire, and authoritarian leadership variously affects a group of children. This article should be read by all teachers who confuse democratic with laissez-faire teaching and who honestly fear giving up some control because they feel chaos will result.

Stouffer, S. A. et al., The American Soldier in World War II: Adjustment During Army Life (Princeton, 1949). This first volume of a series dealing with army life is very relevant for all teachers who are interested in what constitutes effective leadership. Chaps. 5, 7, and 8, especially—although the whole book is worth while—give strong evidence that leadership can make for good or bad morale, and hence poor or good soldiers, more than any other single factor. The book suggests clearly what kind of leaders soldiers—and probably children—most respect. This is an excellent book for teachers who can draw implications from it for the classroom; it is also good reading.

The Teacher's Role in Pupil-Teacher Planning (Teachers College, Columbia University, 1947). This describes in detail just how a teacher can plan daily work with children in the classroom. Stenographic reports of planning periods are presented. Concretely helpful.

Wittenberg, Rudolph M., So You Want to Help People (Association Press, 1947). An excellent manual prepared by the Y.M.C.A. for scout, church, or social groups, presenting a very clear picture of how a group works and how the leader builds good group feeling.

THE ELEMENTARY-SCHOOL YEARS

Hymes, James L., Jr., A Pound of Prevention (New York Committee on Mental Hygiene of the State Charities Aid Association, 1947). This pamphlet discusses how children feel when demands on them are too great. It is especially helpful in dealing with children from homes affected by war, and along with the book by Spock can be read profitably by parents.

Hymes, James L., Jr., *How to Jell Your Child about Sex* (Public Affairs Pamphlet No. 149, 1948). Useful for both parents and teachers who are concerned with sex instruction at any age.

Murphy, Lois B., "Childhood Experience in Relation to Personal Development," in Hunt, J. McV., *Personality and the Behavior Disorders* (Ronald, 1944). Vol. 2. Murphy has written a chapter in Hunt's book which summarizes very well, and in not-too-technical language, studies of children during the elementary-school years.

Redl, Fritz, *Understanding Children's Behavior* (Teachers College, Columbia University, 1949). In this pamphlet Redl attempts with considerable success to translate findings in research into language that is meaningful to teachers and parents. He writes matter-of-factly about problem behavior, causes of behavior, habits, and the adult's feelings toward the child.

Sheviakov, George and Redl, Fritz, *Discipline for Joday's Schools* (National Education Association, 1944). There is probably no other single book which so clearly and effectively explains the "progressive" approach to discipline as does this pamphlet. It discusses not only the reasons for the point of view expressed but also some ways by which the teacher can achieve this kind of control.

ADOLESCENCE

Blanchard, Phyllis, "Adolescent Experience" in Hunt, J. McV., *Personality and the Behavior Disorders* (Ronald, 1944), Vol. 2. This is an excellent, concise discussion of the problems an adolescent faces. It would be difficult to find a more condensed yet not over-simplified psychological description of this age level.

Blos, Peter, *The Adolescent Personality* (Appleton-Century-Crofts, 1941). Blos discusses adolescence by presenting in considerable detail the case studies or histories of four reasonably normal adolescents, two boys and two girls, and then draws implications for all adolescents from these cases. A very absorbing and valuable study which should be read by anyone working with high-school-age children.

High-School Methods with Slow Learners (National Education Association *Research Bulletin*, Oct. 1943). Offers very concrete material for the teacher of the slow learner.

Now Hear Youth: A Report of California Cooperative Study of High School Drop-outs and Graduates (California State Department of Education, 1953). This pamphlet throws considerable light on the question of why high-school students don't like high school and drop out.

Zachry, Caroline B. and Lighty, Margaret, *Emotion and Conduct in Adolescence* (Appleton-Century-Crofts, 1940). The authors have written a clear description of emotional problems during adolescence and use many cases to illustrate their point of view.

LEARNING IN THE CLASSROOM

Buros, Oscar K. (ed.), *The Mental Measurements Yearbooks* (Rutgers, 1949, *et seq.*). Every teacher should be familiar with this volume—which is revised and reissued every few years—and every school should own it or have easy access to it. Buros has collected expert evaluations of almost every kind of test given in the United States today—achievement, intelligence, personality, etc.—and his authors discuss objectively the strengths, weaknesses, uses and limitations of the tests (which are cited by name and publisher). Since it is difficult to tell from advertising just how valuable a test is—and how it can best be used—reference to this volume by anyone giving tests will make for a great saving in time and money and effort.

Developing Programs for Young Adolescents (Association for Supervision and Curriculum Development, 1954). This booklet presents some specific ideas for the junior-high-school curriculum.

Gates, Arthur I. *et al.*, *Educational Psychology* (Macmillan, 1948). This may well be the most comprehensive review of educational psychology. Here the teacher will find a discussion of almost every aspect of learning in the classroom.

Mentally Retarded Students in California Secondary Schools (California State Department of Education, 1953). This bulletin concretely brings together experiences of many people working with the adolescent slow learner in the high-school setting.

Mursell, James L., *Psychological Testing* (Longmans, 1949). Educators who wish to know just what an intelligence test can and cannot measure, as well as the reasons behind and for any other kind of tests, including personality tests, should be familiar with this compact and reasonably thorough book.

Olson, Willard C., *Child Development* (D. C. Heath, 1949). Drawing upon research on development of the total child, Olson discusses among other things how, according to his point of view, learning takes place. Not only is a theory presented but the reader learns of many recent and important researches in this field.

Pratt, Caroline, *I Learn from Children* (Simon & Schuster, 1948). Caroline Pratt was a pioneer "progressive educator" in this country, and in this book she tells the story of her life as a teacher. It is not and is not intended as a scholarly study, and although her ideas cannot be transplanted immediately and totally to all school systems, there are many of her experiences which a teacher may draw upon for help. The book is excellently and vividly written.

STUDYING THE INDIVIDUAL CHILD AND WORKING WITH PARENTS

Bettelheim, Bruno, *Love Is Not Enough* (Free Press, 1950). Bettelheim reports in this book his work with very disturbed, though not necessarily psychotic, children at the Chicago Orthogenic School. Some teachers and parents might find his formulations of genesis and treatment provocative and even applicable, in part, to more usual situations.

D'Evelyn, Katherine E., *Individual Parent-Teacher Conferences* (Teachers College, Columbia University, 1945). D'Evelyn presents perhaps the clearest discussion on how to conduct a parent-teacher conference that can be found. She describes not only general guides but gives verbatim reports of actual conferences. She helps the teacher to avoid dangerous advice-giving. An outstanding book.

Fostering Mental Health in Our Schools. (National Education Association, 1950). This has many excellent chapters on child psychology—although perhaps the one dealing with sociograms should be applied with caution if at all. Chaps. 9, 12, 14, and 18 are especially relevant to the teacher studying a particular child.

Havighurst, R. J., *Developmental Tasks and Education* (Longmans, 1950). The teacher or parent who is puzzled as to whether or not a child's behavior is deviant might find this condensed description of stages of development helpful.

Helping Teachers Understand Children, (American Council on Education, 1945). This publication (see pp. 21*ff.*) is helpful to the teacher who wishes to make anecdotal observations of individual children. There are fine examples of both ineffective or meaningless records and effective and useful records. It is perhaps important to note that it is impossible for most if not all teachers to retain the aloofness and objectivity that the authors advocate, but that teachers should realize that their judgments are likely to change during their careful study of the child and afterwards.

Levy, John and Munroe, Ruth L., *The Happy Family* (Knopf, 1938). Levy and his wife have written the only book on marriage which can be recommended to married couples without fear of creating anxiety in them. Many teachers find this book helpful in their own lives. It is reassuring without being superficial and deals with problems of both marriage and parenthood.

Menninger, William C., *Psychiatry: Its Evolution and Present Status* (Cornell, 1949). Teachers who wish a simple, authoritative, and clear discussion of what psychiatry attempts to do for disturbed individuals will find it in this book. It will clarify many misconceptions about psychiatry and should be read by all teachers who wish to be informed about this companion profession.

Strang, Ruth, *Introduction to Child Study* (Macmillan, 3d. ed., 1951). In this book Strang presents a valuable compendium of information on child development, problem children, methods of working with children, etc.

INDEX